The Diaries of
LORD LIMERICK'S
GRAND TOUR
1716 to 1723

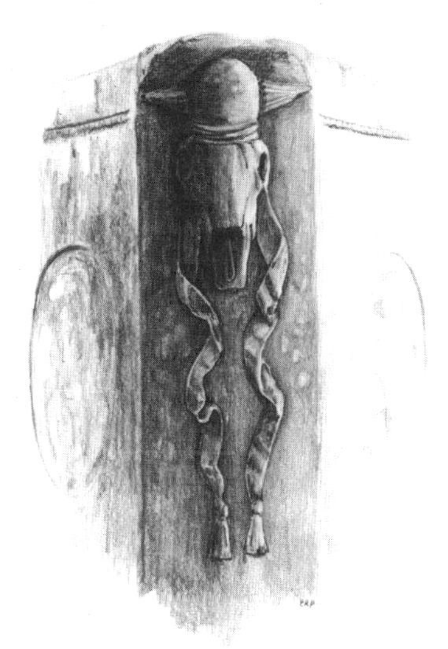

Doon House
Summer Party
2008

Portrait by Francesco Trevisani of Lord Limerick in an embroidered smoking coat and hat.

The Diaries of LORD LIMERICK'S GRAND TOUR 1716 to 1723

EDITED BY THE EARL OF RODEN

First published in the County Louth Archaeological and Historical
Journal, Vol. XXV, No. 3, 2003.

ISBN 0-9539033-1-1

Printed by Dundalgan Press Ltd, Dundalk,
for Doonreaghan Press

Front cover: Travellers in a landscape by Theobold Michau (1676-
                   1765). From Lord Limerick's collection.

Back cover: Lord Limerick's Coat of Arms.

Illustration by: Ebba Kinberg Pate.

Photographs by: Jimmy Green.

CONTENTS

ILLUSTRATIONS

ACKNOWLEDGEMENTS

I would like to thank Vincent and Maribel Slevin, and David Ashton for their Spanish translations, John Leyden of Headfort School for his help with Latin inscriptions, Gerd Riccius, Hélène Hatte and Anne-Marie Reinhardt for uncovering the more obscure aspects of French history, Anthony Malcomson and Diana Scarisbrick. I would also like to acknowledge the generous support of Noel Ross of the County Louth Archaeological and Historical Society. In particular, I would like to thank my wife, Ann, for all her help and advice.

Lord Limerick

When he came of age in 1715, James Hamilton was returned as MP for the borough of Dundalk in Ireland. In 1719, he was created Viscount Limerick and Baron Claneboye and sat in the Irish House of Lords. Subsequently he represented several English constituencies in the British House of Commons. In 1746, he was made a Privy Councillor; he was also Governor of County Louth. He was created Earl of Clanbrassill in 1756, two years before he died. In 1728, he married Harriet Bentinck, sister of the 1st Duke of Portland, in The Hague. Lord Limerick's father, James Hamilton of Tollymore, had purchased a substantial part of Dundalk from the Dungannon family and this was subsequently added to by Lord Limerick's mother, Anne Mordaunt. Lord Limerick rebuilt much of Dundalk and instigated the construction of Dundalk harbour. Although it was not the success he at first envisaged, he is chiefly remembered for his efforts to start the cambric industry in the town, bringing over Huguenot weavers for this purpose.

In addition to his demesne in Dundalk, he developed Tollymore Park on the northern slopes of the Mourne mountains as his summer retreat. As his son had no heir, the family properties passed in turn to his daughter, Anne, who had married the 1st Earl of Roden.

Although he was only created Viscount Limerick in 1719, between his two tours, I have referred to him throughout as Lord Limerick to avoid any confusion.

INTRODUCTION

The great uses of travelling may be comprehended in these few words, to raise in us new ideas, to enlarge the understanding, to cast off all national prejudices, to choose what is eligible in other countries, and to abandon what is bad in our own, and lastly to learn to love our own happy island by comparing the many benefits and blessings we enjoy above any other country and climate in the world.

(Francis Drake, who was in Italy 1750-2.)[1]

Over many centuries there had been considerable travel to and from the Continent, whether it was for commercial ends, military campaigns, diplomatic missions, or salvation. But it was the eighteenth century that witnessed the first widespread travel purely for cultural and pleasure purposes – for those who had the time and resources to do so.

The conflicts and fragile economies of the seventeenth century had forced the élite to conserve their wealth or apply themselves to more serious matters nearer home. Following Marlborough's victories over Louis XIV's France, the suppression of the Jacobite rising and, importantly, the peaceful accession of the Hanoverians, England's attitude towards the Continent underwent a sea change. A new mood of self-confidence became apparent following the 1713 peace agreements. France, for so long England's traditional enemy, even became an ally when Spain reopened hostilities in 1718. It was to be the start of a golden era of the Grand Tour. A few incidental wars mid-century necessitated the odd modification to plans, but travel continued unabated until the watershed of the French Revolution.[2] Napoleon's campaigns then put Italy out of bounds, saw the disintegration of the artist structures in Rome and the commandeering of antiquities for the greater glory of France. Tourism did pick up soon afterwards but with a different emphasis and wider horizons, especially when Greece and the eastern Mediterranean became more accessible.

Given the new environment of the 1720s, leading families encouraged their sons, and sometimes daughters, to travel on the Continent, so much so that it was soon considered *comme il faut* to do a tour. The young scions usually had a tutor, or bearleader, in nominal charge, but people of all ages now began to cross the Channel in increasing numbers, sometimes to the consternation of the English Exchequer. The English and Irish nobility were not the

1 Jeremy Black, *Italy and the Grand Tour* (New Haven and London, 2003).
2 A few adventurous travellers did go to observe armies in action on the Continent – eighteenth-century battlefield tours.

only people seizing this opportunity. While there were more people leaving England than arriving, other countries produced their fair share of tourists, as can be seen from the lists of people Lord Limerick recorded as having met at each major city.

The prime eighteenth-century destination was Paris which, despite the earlier wartime exigencies, was by far the largest European city and a hub of civilisation and art. Rome and the Italian cities offered culture, classical antiquities, collecting, pleasure and a warm climate. With easier access and better roads, the Low Countries were the third most popular destination. However, Spain and Portugal were the prerogative of the more determined and experienced traveller. As England's envoy to Lisbon, Lord Tyrawley, remarked, these two countries 'excite one's curiosity more than any other countries by being least known'.

Most people made for the principal cities and only the more intrepid ventured off the main arterial routes. Poor roads, the likelihood of breakdowns, flea-ridden post houses, currency problems and banditry deterred the average tourist, and besides, the cultural and social hot spots were to be found mainly in the cities. Lord Limerick appears to have taken all the problems associated with provincial travel in his stride, lodging at post houses, inns, large houses or, on one occasion, being forced to sleep on 'hurdles' in a Spanish 'cottage'.

The Grand Tour was generally a protracted and wide-ranging experience lasting in some instances three or more years rather than a specific visit for a singular purpose. While conveniently filling in time for the younger members of the family, it was as much about furthering education and building a foundation for the future. Pure sightseeing and leisure would come later. For those who were likely to play a leading role in their country's affairs, the Grand Tour was an important prerequisite. Contacts at foreign courts and firsthand assessment of the failings and structures of continental countries could prove invaluable, particularly since most countries were probably going to be in dispute or at war with one another in the future, possibly several times over.

The main port of entry to the Continent and the one offering the shortest sea passage was Calais. But there was no roll-on roll-off ferry terminal, or even a harbour, in the early eighteenth century. Ships would anchor offshore and passengers, baggage, tutors and servants would have to disembark into rowing boats, often a hazardous undertaking in choppy seas.

The requirement for passports depended on the state of the country or province to be visited. They were usually obtained from the local governor and had to be shown at most major towns en route, not unlike travelling in the remoter parts of Asia today. Lord Limerick's Spanish passports set out a personal description. He was tall; hair – a wig; beard – thick; distinguishing features – blue eyes (another passport states grey eyes). His age in 1723 is shown as twenty-five. His two servants who accompanied him on his second trip were, well, just servants. With the prevalence of bubonic plague some countries tried to impose a time-consuming, mandatory period of quarantine, as Lord Limerick found out when crossing into Spain.

Post-chaises were available for the run down to Paris, a good two to three days' journeying. An alternative was to buy one's own carriage if travelling further afield and, hopefully, sell it on the return journey, not unlike the ubiquitous Volkswagens that now continuously circumnavigate the Australian outback. The main roads to and from Paris were usually kept in good repair; likewise, the roads over the flat plains of Lombardy, where fifty to eighty kilometres per day was possible. On smaller provincial roads it would be much less. The roads in Spain were notoriously bad and, as in the case of the Alps, the crossing of the Pyrenees was a major undertaking. On his second tour Lord Limerick took just over a month to travel from Paris to Madrid. This included some sightseeing, stoppages for repairs to his carriage, and illness to one of his servants.

Finance was a continual problem for travellers. France's post-war economy was in poor shape and much the same applied to Spain. Currency was often arbitrarily debased and in some areas non-existent. Then again, a *livre* struck in Tours was worth one-fifth less than the *livre parisis* (struck in Paris). The value of coins would also vary depending on the date when struck and some would be more acceptable than others. Credit could be arranged with London bankers in advance and money obtained through their agents, or factors, who were often accused of charging high commissions. Lord Limerick left a list of his financial transactions on his second tour involving loans and advances from agents and other parties. He appears to have managed his finances without undue difficulty at a time when some travellers were forced to return to Paris on account of the precarious financial state of the country. Travel arrangements, lodgings and meals all had to be negotiated on arrival and much depended on availability.

The prevailing mood in the British Isles among the Protestant establishment at the beginning of the eighteenth century was anti-Catholic, and many travelling to the Continent did so with misgivings or suspicion. As Jeremy Black makes the point in his excellent book on the Grand Tour,[3] it was not unlike travelling to Russia and China at the height of the Cold War. However, once war had been concluded with France and the Jacobites and Irish duly suppressed, the Establishment breathed a little easier, more so when Parliament endorsed the Protestant succession to the English throne. Nevertheless there was still a certain amount of unease, especially where Jacobites were given succour and bases in some continental cities. Many commentators, Lord Limerick included, reckoned that the power of the

---

3 Jeremy Black, *The British Abroad, The Grand Tour in the Eighteenth Century* (Stroud, 1992).

French monarchy was too great and the state of the country evidence of the drawbacks of absolutism. Likewise, the religious autocracy and the questionable methods used to ensure the subservience of the populace drew further criticism. This engendered a censure of the Catholic religion or, at times, ridicule, especially on the matter of superstitions, indulgences and the power of relics. This is understandable when a new thinking on church and state was being propounded by philosophers such as Locke and Kilkenny-born Bishop Berkeley. Attracted by this new outlook, Voltaire, whom Lord Limerick met in Brussels, later chose London as a stopping-place on his ceaseless exile from conservative France. With the eclipse of the Jacobite movement and the ending of the Seven Years War in 1763, religious tensions were less of an issue for travellers on the Continent.

There are many entries in the Diaries recording visits to 'convents' (abbeys), cathedrals or nunneries, and meetings with priests, some of them Irish. Furthermore, it appears that Lord Limerick was generally well received by these institutions and individuals. It was probably as a result of his observations on these tours that he decided at a later date to put forward a parliamentary bill for the regulation of the Irish priesthood and the establishment of a properly constituted seminary as an alternative to what could become a coercive, underground movement. In his presentation he stated that: 'I have long wished for the opportunity to reconcile, if possible, the Papists of this Country to our happy Constitution, and their own true interest, and to turn a loose, indiscriminate, illegal Connivance into a regular, restrained, legal Toleration'. His bill passed the Commons but was rejected by the Privy Council. It was only after the religious colleges in France attended by aspiring Irish students were destroyed during the French Revolution that Maynooth was founded in 1795.

News from the Continent at the end of the seventeenth century would have been eagerly awaited in the Hamilton household. After all, Lord Limerick's father had been active in his support for King William at the Battle of the Boyne. *La Gloire* of Louis XIV and the most powerful country in Europe was at its apogee. France had extended her borders to include much of Flanders and territories as far as the Rhine. An invasion of England had been narrowly averted by the loyalty and seamanship of Admiral Russell who, along with the Dutch fleet, destroyed the French naval armada at Cape Le Hogue in 1692. But if Louis' ambitions for England had been dashed, there were other fruits ripening and waiting to be picked. In 1701, Charles II of Spain died childless. One of his sisters had married Louis XIV, the other the Austrian emperor. Both had sons and a plan was hatched to carve up the Spanish empire much to the valid concerns of the Spaniards. On his death-bed the disease-ravaged Charles signed a will solely in favour of the Duke of Anjou, Louis XIV's grandson, believing this would ensure the continuation of his empire. A turning point in France's destiny arrived hotfoot (or rather on horseback) from the Escorial. Would Louis stand by his earlier agreements to share the Spanish spoils or go for the jackpot on his own? Greed was to be his and ultimately France's downfall. Misjudging the reaction of 'Les Goddams' (English) and the Austrians, Louis confirmed acceptance of the will announcing to the weary Spanish ambassador that 'The Pyrenees are no more!'. Little did he know that there would follow a great deal more war.

To start with everything went well for France. Back in Madrid the Duke of Anjou was duly proclaimed Philip V of Spain with the support of most but not all the country's provinces. Louis was welcomed by the commander in the Spanish Netherlands (largely present-day Belgium) and the string of Dutch-controlled forts and strongholds passed to France with hardly a flintlock being fired. Even the Jacobites thought that their time had come (again) and when James II died the year after Charles, Louis recognised his son as the king of England. The touch-paper had well and truly been lit and the War of the Spanish Succession, which few participants really wanted, began. The powerful Duke of Marlborough plunged into the heart of France inflicting, initially, defeat after humiliating defeat on her forces until at last the Treaty of Utrecht, a series of agreements between the main protagonists, brought matters to a conclusion in 1713.

The young Lord Limerick, about to study law at Oxford, now witnessed a vastly changed Europe. Philip V was allowed to hold on to all of Spain and the Indies. France acknowledged the Protestant succession in Britain and expelled the Old Pretender[4] (to Rome). England retained Gibraltar and thus control of the Mediterranean. The Dutch got their forts back and the Austrian Empire absorbed what had been the Spanish Netherlands. Portugal, for its limp service to the allied cause, obtained what turned out to be lucrative trading rights in Brazil.

Although Lord Limerick first visited France three years after Utrecht, the effects of the war were clearly visible. France's finances were in a perilous condition. The slaughter in recent battles like Malplaquet would only be equalled in Napoleon's campaigns, while south of the Pyrenees Spain begrudged the needless loss of her possessions, which the enfeebled Charles had fondly thought he was protecting for posterity. It was a grudge that led to renewed hostilities taking place between the time of Lord Limerick's first visit to France and his visit to Spain.

At the beginning of the seventeenth century, Spain's army had been the finest in the world and her navy one of the largest. At the close the latter was annihilated and the army only able to establish a monarchy of sorts with the aid of France, all largely due to the corruption of power and court intrigues. Philip V, the first Bourbon king of Spain, was twice driven out of his capital

---

4 The Old Pretender, James Stuart, (1688-1766), took part in the ill-conducted Scottish rebellion led by the Earl of Mar before fleeing in 1715. As France had been closed to him following the Treaty of Utrecht, he was forced to go to Rome where he became the darling of the impecunious exiles.

during the war and lost Valencia and Barcelona to the English under the Earl of Peterborough, Lord Limerick's uncle on his mother's side.

Spain's main grievance with the Treaty of Utrecht was the loss of Sicily and Naples to Austria, and Gibraltar to the English, plus the fact that English freebooters were carving up the Spanish American trade and Philip was unable to do anything about it. Cardinal Alberoni, Spain's chief minister, had been granted five years by his king to rebuild the country. To this end he was largely successful but Spain was by no means ready for further hostilities. Before Alberoni had completed his task, an impatient Philip decided to invade Sardinia and Sicily. Unfortunately for Spain the English navy under Admiral Bynge destroyed the Spanish fleet at Cape Passaro in 1718 and the venture ended in failure. Louis XIV died the year before Lord Limerick's first visit to France, and Philip resigned his throne a year after Limerick's tour of Spain.

Given the campaigns that had taken place just prior to Lord Limerick's tours, it is not surprising that there are numerous observations in his diaries about the state of European armies and fortifications. But his interests were wide-ranging, encompassing architecture, landscape, gardens and forestry, religion, taxation and revenue, history and education. It can be assumed that his observations were just as much for his own record as for family and friends at home.

The first tour in the early summer of 1716 down the Loire valley was a short trip (by Grand Tour standards) lasting just under a month. His mode of travel on this occasion was post-chaise or river boat. It appears he cut his journey short and returned abruptly to Paris, probably to start his tour to Italy. Sadly, the Italian diary, if he kept one, has been lost. But we do know that he was in Padua on 20 December 1716.[5] He had his portrait painted by the much sought-after artist, Francesco Trevisani, who was working in Rome at that time and didn't work outside Italy. There is also a reference to the Alps in his later Spanish diary. This tour started in the summer of 1722. Leaving Calais, Lord Limerick went first to Brussels and then Spa, where he paused for a few weeks, possibly taking the waters there and in the neighbouring 'springs'. From Brussels he went to Paris before taking the direct route to Bordeaux. Crossing the Pyrenees at Bayonne, he made straight for Madrid. It was now mid-winter and he stayed two months in or near Madrid. Some of his brief historical entries whilst in Madrid could well have been date-fillers waiting for the weather to clear. Most of the people he recorded as meeting in Madrid were women.

From Madrid he went directly to Lisbon, staying a month in Portugal before re-entering southern Spain and heading for Cadiz and Gibraltar. After reaching Malaga he went inland to Cordoba and Grenada. From Grenada he

---

5 John Ingamells (compiler), *A Dictionary of British and Irish Travellers in Italy 1701-1800* (New Haven and London, 1997).

headed due east crossing the kingdom of Murcia before arriving in Alicante on 23 April. Here his diary ceases. The note book is full to the last page and it would seem likely that he did continue the journal. We know from the account of his finances and his passport that he was in Barcelona on 15 May. One passport, issued in Cataluna, an area still smarting from the recent upheavals, granted him and his servants 'free and safe' passage into France accompanied by an escort of four cavalrymen for 'his personal security'. Once across the Pyrenees he probably made his way home via Paris and Calais, selling his carriage to an incoming tourist as he left France. Five years later Lord Limerick was back on the Continent, this time for his marriage in The Hague to Harriet Bentinck.

In the second diary Lord Limerick's observations are those of a more seasoned traveller. He was also better organised having his own coach, two servants and, according to his passport, two suitcases of luggage. His interests now extended to 'antiquities', presumably resulting from his sojourn in Italy. However, his views on baroque architecture were not that enthusiastic. The monastery at La Cartuja, one of Spain's most lavish baroque churches, he dismissed as 'nothing remarkable'. In contrast, he considered the new Gothic cathedral in Grenada 'one of the handsomest in Spain'. His interest in Gothic architecture would appear to have developed during this visit. Twenty years later he came into contact with the architect, Thomas Wright of Durham, who was developing his own ideas on the new Gothic-revival architecture, and prevailed upon him to come over to Ireland. The architectural styles of his Irish properties at Dundalk in Co Louth and Tollymore in Co Down may well have germinated in that second part of his Grand Tour.[6]

An additional barrier between the continental countries and England was the different calendars in use at that time. England conformed to the old system that was eleven days behind the Gregorian calendar until the reform in 1752 brought them both into line. Presumably Lord Limerick used the continental calendar during his tours.

I have retained Lord Limerick's original spelling but have changed some of his punctuation, adding missing words in brackets to make the diaries more readable. They are contained in three plain note books and appear to have been written up during his journeys when time and opportunity allowed. The first book covers the trip down the Loire, the second his journey from Calais to Madrid and the third that from Madrid onwards. The Italian diaries, assuming they existed, would have been interesting, as it was in Italy that Lord Limerick, and his son Lord Clanbrassill after him, did most of their collecting. All that Lord Limerick appears to have brought back from Spain are a number of books and an indulgence!

6 The Earl of Roden, *Tollymore, The Story of an Irish Demesne*, published by the Ulster Architectural Heritage Society.

The diaries provide a spontaneous, firsthand compendium of Lord Limerick's travels on the Continent and are thus of greater interest than the distilled travel literature of that time. More importantly, the observations and content give a fuller insight than any other contemporary portrayal into Lord Limerick, the man and his character.

THE FIRST TOUR, 1716

May 30th 1716. I left Paris. On my way to Fontainbleau I passed several fine seats lying upon the Seine. All of them have avenues that reach to the road and most of them handsome parks. There is one of them (that) belong'd to the Duchess of Portsmouth[7] which she sold a little before I went into England. There is also a fine house of the Duke D'Antin[8] halfway between Paris and Fontainbleau called Petitbourg. The King of France us'd always to lye there in his way to Fontainbleau.[9] There is an avenue of five or six leagues in the Paris road that leads to the Palace.[10] The town is situated in the middle of the forest which is fifteen leagues round. There is a small park, or rather a large garden, within the forest that is walled in. It is beautified with very fine hedges and a noble canal that reaches almost the whole length of it. There is a place they call the Meadow in it that is full of fountains. The King used to bring all his court to a fountain in the park where he had order'd little fish to be put to see them catch'd and eat(en) by a crane. At the head of a long canal, between the garden and the park, is a pretty cascade; and in the parterre is a handsome waterwork called the Rock. Beside the canal in the park there is another just before the house in the middle of which there is a summer house where the Dauphin often made entertainments after the King was gone to Bed. 'Tis here the carps so much talked about are kept. The King always fed them himself the day he came to, and the day he left, Fontainbleau and, as they told us, would find out anyone that was missing, tho' there are four hundred of them.

The House has nothing to recommend it but its bigness.[11] There are 360 chambers in it. The King's apartment and that of Madame de Berry are handsome. There are also three handsome Galleries. One of them is full of stags horns; there are 48 of them. As for the rest of the House it is very indifferent. The chappel has nothing extraordinary in it. This House was begun by Francis the First and every King since him has made some addition to it. The

---

7 The Duchess of Portsmouth was Louise de Kerouillac, the beguiling French mistress of Charles II, who was persuaded by Louis XIV to go to London.

8 Duc d'Antin was the son of Louis XIV and Madame de Montespan. Petitbourg is at Evry some 20 km south-east of Paris. Rebuilt in the nineteenth century for a banker, it was burnt by the Germans in 1944.

9 The king was Louis XIV who had died the year previously. He had outlived his son and grandson. His great grandson, the Dauphin, would duly become Louis XV but in the meantime the profligate Regency under Philippe, Duc d'Orléans sowed the seeds for the miseries that were to follow at the end of the century.

10 A league was approximately 3 miles.

11 Fontainebleau, some 55 km south-east of Paris, was the sporting-palace of the kings of France. Originally founded by Robert the Good in the tenth century it was, indeed, added to and embellished by succeeding monarchs. Later, Voltaire accused Madame de Berry's daughter, the Duchesse de Berry, of incest with the Regent which promptly led to Voltaire's exile – thus his meeting with Lord Limerick in Brussels.

building of each King is marked with the first letter of his name. Louis built three Hermitages in the forest.[12] One of them was pulled down by reason of the Hermit being murdered there. The other two are still standing, both of which I saw. The late King used to give entertainments to the Ladys at one that is situated in the wildest place that can be imagin'd. A Hungarian, that had a pension from the King, has writ sentences out of the Bible upon a vast number of rocks in the forest.

June 1st. I went in my chaise to the rendezvous where the Count de Thoulouse[13] came between 11 and 12. The stag was killed about 4 and was given to the Dogs in the Evening. As is constantly done, the Huntsmen keep the Dogs off from the stag with their whips till they are all in a circle then they let them fall on (it). They play on the french horn all the while the Dogs are eating. The English company I met here was Mr Plunket, and his Lady, Capt. Roberts and his wife. I lodged at the St Claude.

June 2nd. After having seen the Palace I went to Montargis where I dined. The Castle of this place belongs to the Regent.[14] There are a great many handsome rooms in it, but all unfurnished. The Hall is the largest room I have seen anywhere. Over the chimney is the picture of the Dog fighting with his master's murderer before one of the Kings of Francc.[15] 'Tis said to have been done in that Hall. They have the Duke of Bedford's standard in this town. He was Regent of France for Harry the Sixth and was oblig'd to raise the siege of this town by reason of sudden inundations; and so lost his standard which they carry about with great pomp once a year. There is a mock fight that day where, after the English are beaten, they give an Entertainment that they call the English feast. Colonel Ingram was the only Englishman I saw here. After Dinner I went on to Lory, and the next day I came to Orleans. I paid 45 livres for horses from Montargis thither. Between Lory[16] and Orleans is a handsome seat belonging to one of the King's Secretaries, Monsieur de la Vrilliere. It is called Chateauneuf. The Gardens are large and well laid out. The Loire runs at the feet of them. Between this and Orleans we crossed the canal that joins the Loire and ye Seine.

12 Hermitages became a popular feature in early eighteenth-century landscape design. That built at Tollymore, Co Down by Lord Limerick's son, Lord Clanbrassill, was more for shelter, contemplation and conversation. In some other parks, and at Fontainebleau, owners endeavoured to create the complete hermitical replica.

13 The Comte of Toulouse (Thoulouze) was the son of Louis XIV and Madame de Montespan. He had a distinguished naval career, particularly during the War of the Spanish Succession.

14 Phillipe, Duc d'Orléans.

15 In 1371 occurred the renowned combat between the dog of Montagis and Macaire, its master's murderer. The dog not only found the spot where its master was buried, but singled out his murderer. Charles VI granted the ordeal of battle to test the murderer's guilt.

16 Present day Lorris, half way between Montagis and Orléans. In today's terms a livre could be worth anything between 1 and 3 Euro.

Orleans stands very pleasantly. It is situated upon the Loire. The University there was formerly very famous for the study of law but has, at present, lost much of its reputation.[17] There are no buildings remarkable but the Cathedral,[18] which is said to have been built by the English. Two of the entrances in fact were repaired by the late King. It is kept very well within. There is a handsome walk here that they call the Mall. The walls round the town are still standing, tho' some of the towers are fallen down.

June 7th. I went about two leagues out of the town to see a place called La Source. The quantity of water that boils up there is so great that boats come up to the very head of the spring. When Gaston of France[19] came there he order'd it to be fathomed, but the depth of the place and the force of the water rising made it impracticable. In the Afternoon I walk'd round the town and saw the figure of the Maid of Orleans upon the Bridge. She is kneeling to the Virgin Mary who has got our Saviour on her lap on one side, and the Dauphin of France on the other. They are both in armour.

June 8th. I came to Blois.[20] On my way I call'd at Clery where there is a tomb of Louis 11th. His figure is kneeling in a praying posture. He is cover'd with a large mantle stuck full of fleur de lis. This monument was put up in 1622, the old one being fall'n down.

June the 9th. I went to the Ursulines[21] to see a nun take the habit. During the sermon the future would-be nun sat directly opposite the Preacher dressed very handsomely in Black. As soon as the sermon was over she came forward to the grate, with a wax candle in her hand, where there were three priests in very rich capes that performed the office. After part of the prayers were over she was conducted out to have her hair cut off and to be dress'd in the habit. After this was done she came again to the grate where they put on the forehead cloth and the veil; and then the curtain was drawn.

In the afternoon I went to the Bishop's palace. It stands very finely on the side of a Hill that overlooks the town and the Loire. The house was built by the present Bishop who was a great favourite of Mme Maintenon.[22] There is a house that he has built behind his for those persons that are to be ordained to live in sometime before (their) ordination. He was stopp'd in his going on with ye building by the King's death. There are two handsome terraces one above the other upon a level with two of the apartments of the house. This

17 Lord Limerick had recently studied law at Oxford.

18 The cathedral was begun in 1278 but subsequently destroyed. Reconstruction by Henry IV began in 1601.

19 Gaston, Duc d'Orléans was the younger brother of Louis XIII. Until Louis managed to conceive a son, who was born in 1638, Gaston was the presumptive heir to the throne.

20 An historic town on the Loire.

21 An order founded by St Angela Merici in 1537 at Brescia to tend the poor and sick, and for the instruction of children.

22 Mistress and later the second wife of Louis XIV. She died in 1719.

place was erected into a Bishoprick in favour of this Gentleman by the late King. The Cathedral of this town is but an indifferent one. The Jesuits have a neat church here. There is an old Castle in this town belonging to the King. The Queen of Poland dyed in it last winter. The figure of one of the Kings of France on horseback is over the Gate. There is a *corps de logis*[23] built by Gaston of France who would have made it all uniform if he had lived. When the Duke of Orleans was building here he wou'd have had the Religious – I think they are Capuchins – of a neighbouring convent pull down a steeple that obstructed his view which, they refusing to do, he threatened to plant a cannon against it. But one of them that was wiser than the rest came to him and told him that they begg'd leave of his Highness to let the steeple stand till the Palace was finished, and that whenever that was done they would immediately pull it Down, which the Duke, not knowing how to refuse, said they had trick'd him but that he must agree to it. He has built a Gallery[24] near the Castle. It is two hundred yards in length. There is a walk just without the town called the Promenade d'Angleterre.

I forgot to mention a convent of Chartreuse that is at Orleans. I went to see it on June ye 5th. It was formerly a Hospital but Louis the 13th – I think – gave it to the Carthusians. The building is very neat and pretty. Their cells open into a Gallery that runs along the garden. Their number in all is twenty four but there are not cells for half of them. They have each of them a handsome room – in the wall of which the bed stands – a study, an oratoire, a Gallery, and a little garden. The Father, who we saw, told us that (on) Sundays and holidays they eat together and were allow'd to talk with one another till vespers. They choose their own Prior unless the place happens to become vacant during the sitting of the General Chapter which lasts but 8 days every year. If he does not behave himself as he ought, they complain and he is turn'd out. They build their cells at this convent as fast as they can get the money; each cell costs ten thousand livres.

June 10th. I went to Chambord[25] about four leagues of Blois. It was built by Francis ye First and designed for a hunting seat. There is a *corps de logis* within the Quadrangle consisting of four towers and a double staircase in the middle. There are four Halls at every landing place so that there are twelve Halls and twelve apartments in the four towers. There is a fine prospect from the top of the Castle. The late King had been here three or four times while the Queen lived, but he never came after her death. The Theatre, where some of Moliere's plays were first acted, is still standing; 'tis in one of the Halls joining to the staircase. There is a forest and Park here.

23 The central structure of a building.

24 Gallery in this instance would have been an arcade or passageway, possibly covered or partly covered.

25 One of the grandest of the Loire chateaux. Moliere's play first performed there was *Bourgeois Gentilhomme,* an attack on bourgeois pretensions.

I met with Mr Darcy, Mr Moore, Mr Morgan, Mr Napper and two more English Gentlemen at Orleans where I lodg'd at ye Three Emperours.

At Blois I met only with Mr Campion. We lodg'd there at the Galley. The horses from Orleans to Blois cost me eighteen livres;[26] and half of the boat from Blois to Tours 10 (livres).

June ye 13th. I set out from Blois and got to Amboise. The country of the right hand of the river is full of vineyards, and the left hand is covered with corn. The only thing remarkable here is an old Castle built several times by the Kings of France. I saw the famous pair of horns in a chappel here. They are twelve foot long and eight wide. They show'd us the place where a bit had been saw'd off for the King of Spain and his Brothers as they pass'd by. 'Twas here Charles the 8th[27] fell dead as he was looking at some of his Courtiers playing Tennis. There are two towers up which the Kings of France used to drive with their coaches. The ascent is made winding round the tower; one of them joins to the King's apartment. In the late Civil Wars of France[28] the Governour of this Castle broke down part of each ascent for fear of being surpris'd. The forest of Amboise – as the man told us – is 25 leagues round. During the last war there were a great many prisoners of war here. I lodg'd here at the Cheval Bardé.

June 14th. I got to Tours which is the handsomest town upon the Loire. The streets are narrow but some of the Houses are handsome enough. The Cathedral is large but indifferently kept. There are two very handsome walks here, one above the other, where all the company of the town meets before supper. They have a new Gate here with the usual inscription *Lu: Clovico Magno*.[29] I lodged at the Galley here. Assemblys are very frequent in this town and, before the scarcity of money, (people) play'd deep here.[30]

June 16th. I went to see a place about two leagues from Tours that is called La Cave Goutiere. They pretend that it goes a great way under ground. We went in at one opening and came out at another about threescore yards of it. The water is continually dropping in most parts of it from icicles that hang on the roof. In many parts of it, where the water flows pretty abundantly, there are large stones formed by the cold that congeal them. The stones are very hard

26 Orléans to Blois is 56 km.

27 Charles VIII died at Amboise in 1498, aged 28, having struck his head on a lintel. Enthralled by what he saw during his successful campaign in Italy he was responsible for bringing Renaissance art to France.

28 It was the War of the Fronde 1648-53 from which the young Louis XIV emerged all powerful and in total control of France. ('L'etat, c'est moi!').

29 Clovis, a Frankish king, liberated Tours from the Visigoths in AD 505. Encouraged by his wife, Clothilde, he became a Christian but only after he had called on her patron saint to bring him victory in a battle that looked like going very much against him.

30 France had become almost bankrupt thanks largely to Louis XIV's military adventures. The resulting shortage of money often caused problems for travellers. To 'play deep' was to gamble for high stakes. The opiate of the French nobility, gambling was much encouraged by the king.

and as white as snow. I brought away some pieces that our guide broke with a hammer. In one place the water Bubbles up as out of a jet d'eau.

June 19th. I went to see a convent where the saint lyes buried that founded the Mission of St Francis de Salles.[31] The History of his life is painted round the cloister. They show'd us several rich habits that had been presented to them by the Kings of France. They have a pleasant garden. The Friar told me that Touraine[32] brought a greater revenue into the crown than any province in France except Normandy. I think he said the crown received as much again as the land let out of that province. They have a neat chappel here. There is an inscription round the tomb of their founder signifying that his body was taken up by Heretics and that the remains only were there of what they could pick up. There are a great many trinkets hung up here. From hence I went to Marmoutier, a famous convent of the Benedictines. The church is large but has nothing remarkable in it. There is only one wing of the building finish'd, which is very handsome. They have three storeys but the cells are not double as in most convents. Their refectory is a handsome old building. 'Twas built by one of the Queens of England – William the Conquerer's wife as I remember. From thence we went to an old chappel where they show'd us the graves of the Seven Sleepers. After they had slept several years St Anthony, as our guide informed us, desired leave of God to waken them, which accordingly he did, and bid them prepare for death for they should live but a month, which happen'd as foretold.

June 20th. I hir'd horses for 8 livres a day and got to Richlieu[33] that night where the Duke of that name has a fine Palace. The gardens are run to ruin, but the house is in very good order. The two wings of the house were built by the last Cardinal but the body of the house is much older. There are a great many good antique statues here that the Cardinal had sent for out of Italy, and some good pictures. The town is the neatest and most regular that can be seen anywhere. It was built by (the townspeople) that belong'd to the Cardinal to make their court to him. It is free of all dutys at the entrance of the town.

June 21st. I left Richlieu and din'd at Chinon under a ruin'd Castle that is there. There are cellars that run in a great way under ground, at least two hundred yards. From hence I went along the side of a river that falls into the Loire to Saumur where we lodged at the Three Moors. There is nothing worth seeing but the Castle that commands a view of the Province of Anjou, and a convent of the Peres de l'Oratoire. One of the altars in their chappel,

---

31 St Francis of Sales (1562-1622) was a French bishop and one of the leaders of the Counter-Reformation.

32 Touraine, or the Department of Indre-et-Loire, is the district with Tours at its centre.

33 Richelieu was the first planned town in France, built under the supervision of the cardinal. The palace was demolished in 1805. Richelieu was Louis XIII's first minister and one of France's greatest statesmen. He commissioned Nicolas Poussin to paint the landscapes that made his early reputation.

that is dedicated to the Virgin Mary, has this inscription on it; *Filia Dei Patris, Mater Dei Filii Spousa Spiritus Sancti.*

The 23rd. I went to see the Abbey of Fontevrault.[34] The Abbess of this convent is the Governess of all that order. There are 250 nuns here, and there are two hundred priests belonging to the convent, most of whom the Abbess sends to those convents she has the Government of so that there are not above 50 or 60 commonly resident there; but they are all obliged to pay their homage once a year to the abbess when she appoints them what they are to do. The two convents are both enclosed with the same wall, tho' they are divided from one another afterwards. The present Lady Abbess is a niece of Madam Montespan's. They have had abbesses of the Bourbon family. Mr le Duc has two sisters there, one profess'd and the other a pensioner only. I saw one Mr Cusac, an Irish priest, there but didn't know who he was until afterwards.

The 27th. In the evening I took post for Angers[35] and got there late at night. I saw the Queen of Sicily's cage out of which she would not stir after her Husband had imprison'd her for six years there, but lived there six years more of her own accord, going out only to chappel. A criminal that was shut up there some few years ago broke his way out, tho' one wou'd think it almost impossible.

June 28th. I left this (place) in order to return to Paris. I had met here with Mr Mansel and Mr Bartie. I din'd that day at La Flèche where Harry the Fourth[36] built a very handsome college for the Jesuits.

THE SECOND TOUR, 1722-3

JULY 1722.

4th. The long gun in Dover castle was given by the States[37] to Queen Elizabeth after the defeat of the Spanish armada. It is 24 foot 2 inches long and carries seven mile and a quarter. It takes 15 pound of powder to charge it.

6th. I was about nine hours in crossing to Calais in a market-boat of twenty tun.

34 The abbey of Fontevrault was founded in 1099. The order was governed by an abbess who was subject only to the pope. The order, which included both nuns and priests, was abolished during the French Revolution. The 'convent' subsequently became a major prison before being restored.

35 Angers is 110 km west of Tours and 300 km south-west of Paris. The queen of Sicily mentioned by Limerick is possibly Yolande d'Aragon who married Louis of Anjou in 1400. A renowned beauty, she played a prominent role in French politics for over forty years before spending the last years of her life in Angers.

36 Henry of Navarre succeeded his cousin Henry III. Unable to subjugate Paris in the Wars of Religion, he became a Catholic ('Paris is worth a Mass'). He established religious freedom throughout France following the Edict of Nantes in 1598, but was assassinated by a Catholic fanatic (as was his cousin) in 1610.

37 The States was the parliament of the Netherlands. The Dutch had fought Spain to a standstill concluding an armistice in 1609.

18th. The Recolets[38] have a handsome new church at Gravelines.

19th. From Ghent to Brussels is all paved.

20th. The Theatre at Brussels is very large. There are five rows of boxes.

22nd. The roads from Brussels to Liège are almost entirely in a direct line. The country is not so flat as on the other side of Brussels, but is agreeably varied by little risings, villages and coppices.

23rd. The country between Liège and Spa is very mountainous and full of steep ascents and descents. The mountaineers look like a different species from those in the flat country.

24th. Spa is surrounded on every side by hills cover'd with wood(s) that seem to hang over it. The buildings are very indifferent and fitted barely for a summer accommodation for strangers. Spa is in the territory of Liège. There are several mineral springs, hardly known, in all parts of the adjacent country. About three leagues from Spa there is a cascade that falls about forty feet.

At Brussels – Mr Cole, Role and Daniel.

At Spa – Mr Mansel, Cottington, Hobart, Dickinson, Robarts, Gillord and Rotten.

AUGUST

21st. Chaudefontaine[39] is about five leagues from Spa and two from Liège. The water there is blood warm. Liège is situated on the Meuse. The town-house that was fired when the French bombarded the town, is just finish'd and handsomely rebuilt. There is but one regiment of about eight hundred men kept by this State.

22nd. The Bishop of Liège is chose(n) by the Canons of St Lambert who are sixty besides the Bishop. The Canons are nam'd by the Emperor,[40] the Pope, the Bishops and the University of Louvain. Each of them has three months in the year, and the name to the Canonrys that fall vacant in that time. This is a mistake. The university of Louvain has but two months, March and November. The Pope has four, but he has given them up to the Bishop so that he has now ten months. There are besides seven other chapters in Liège, the canons of which are named after the same manner. They say there are four and twenty towns, eighteen Bourgs, and seventeen hundred villages in the territory of Liège. Their taxes are light, that upon malt is the heaviest. Publick houses pay no more towards it than private ones. The Butcher's meat sold in the town is tax'd. A beef pays six escalines,[41] a calf or a sheep two. Hops which grow in great number near the town, are not tax'd unless they are carried out of the country. They are sold this year for twenty eight escalines the hundred

---

38   Another name for the Franciscans. Gravelines is halfway between Calais and Dunkirk.

39   The mineral springs at Chaudfontaine reach 92 degrees Fahrenheit.

40   The emperor of Austria who 'acquired' Belgian territory in the Treaty of Utrecht.

41   An escalin was worth an English shilling of the time.

pounds weight. They reckon an hundred thousand people in Liège. The country is very well peopled too. The view of the town from the Carthusian convent is very agreeable. It stands upon the side of a hill about half a mile from the town and the plain between it and the river is one continued hop garden.

23rd. Louvain is four leagues from Brussels, a large town not well-built.

31st. The dearest article in housekeeping at Brussels is fire, every thing else is very cheap.

At Brussels – Mr Chambers, Guthrie, Weldon, Swinburn, Worth, Mansel, Frazer, Hay, Robarts, Darcy, Plunkett, Comte Castelbares, C. de la Tour, C. Nava, C. Batatti, P. Escolas, Marquis de los Rios, Marechal Vehlen, Mon. de Weiden, le Fevre, Cuvigny, de la Cour, Prince de la Tour, Baron d'Ogny, Baron d'Hourse, Mon. Sandrin, Milben, Kairmin, Rousseau,[42] Voltaire, Negrette, P. de Ventimigglia. C. Lanoy, Mar. D'yase.

SEPTEMBER

3rd. The part of Brussels that was bombarded by the late French King[43] is handsomely rebuilt with brick, but the buildings of the other parts are mostly wood. An officer, or soldier, in the Emperor's service can only be try'd by his proper officers for any crime, tho' he shou'd be absent from his regiment, unless they appoint others to do it.

20th. The best Brussels tapistry costs three pistoles a yard square. In the P: de la Tour's family they use five and forty pound of tea in a month. The regiments of the Low Countries do not have the same privileges of the German regiments. All officers in the German services, from the highest to the lowest, are paid by a certain number of soldier's portions.

21st. The Emperor's territories are separated from the French about three leagues from Valenciennes by a little rivulet. The country from Mons to Valenciennes is not so well wooded as Brabant.

24th. From Valenciennes to Cambray[44] there is hardly a tree to be seen. The Cittadel of Cambray was one of the first built in the Low Countries. It is a square and is situated on a rising ground so that it commands the town entirely. The town is very ill-built, chiefly with wood faced with slates. In the middle of the great place there is a chappel not four yards square that is worth eight thousand livres a year to its priest who says mass there at four a clock every morning. The Cathedral is an old clumsy building. The choir is

---

42 The Rousseau mentioned here is probably the poet, Jean-Baptiste, who had spoken up for Voltaire when he was exiled by the Regent. Jean-Jacques Rousseau would have only been eleven at the time.

43 Brussels was bombarded by Marechal Villeroi during the War of the Spanish Succession destroying over 400 houses.

44 Cambrai was taken by the Spaniards in 1595 but ceded to France by the Treaty of Nimegen in 1678.

newly fitted up. No part of what they call the pays conquis pays the taille.[45] The other taxes are the same as the other taxes in the rest of France. From Cambray to Peronne is a bare country. After Peronne one sees coppices scatter'd on rising grounds but there is no great wood till one comes to the forest of Chantilly.

At Cambray – M. de St Coutest, C. St Ethevan, M. Beretti, C. Windisgrats, B. Bentenreider, CC. Didrichstein, C. Provana, C. St Severin.

L. Polwarth, L. Binning, Sr. Arthur Haslerig, M. Sutton, Bondeau, de Villere, Hume, Stuart, Scot, Payn.

OCTOBER

12th. I left Paris. Four posts and a half is the little town of Arpajon, formerly Chatre,[46] but the Marquis d'Arpajon has changed the name of it. Between this place and Estrechy is a hill something steep, but not a high one. At the top of it is a little hovel with a great number of poles which serve instead of drags for the carts that pass. They pay each of them three pence. The person it belongs to lets the stand for five hundred livres a year. Most of the carts hereabouts are on two wheels placed almost in the middle of the carriage. Estampes is a little town, ill-built. It has an old wall with towers round it. There are a good many vineyards between that and Paris and the country is well wooded. But from Estampes to Toury there is hardly a vineyard and the country is bare of wood. At Toury I lay at the Grand Cerf.

13th. A good part of the way from Toury to Orleans lies thro' forest. Most of the vineyards are on the bank of the Loire. At La Ferté there is a very large seat that belong'd to the Marechal of that name.[47] It lies low but the gardens are handsome and the avenue is long. I lay at the post-house at Romorentin which belongs to the D. of Orleans. It is the capital of Solonge which is an indifferent country.

14th. At two leagues from Romorentin I crossed the Cher in a boat. This river divides Solonge from Berry, which seems to be no fine country. There is a good deal of wood and corn in it, vineyards in some parts, but the wine is not good. The soil is light, yet I saw in one place five youk of oxen to a very small plow. They were little indeed. I lay at Argenton at the post-house.

15th. Argenton is a little town ill-built as are all those I have seen in Berry. It belongs to the Duke of Orleans. It lies in a bottom. The hills about are cover'd with vineyards that produce coarse wine. The most substantial people of the town are Protestants. There runs a little river thro' it. I was forced to stay there for the mending of my chaise.

---

45 The taille was an unpopular land tax largely borne by the peasantry and new bourgeoisie, the nobility being exempt.

46 Chatre, not to be confused with Chartres, is 30 km south-west of Paris.

47 Marechal La Ferté was involved in the rebuilding of Lorraine after the Thirty Years War. La Ferté is a charming chateau, still with its substantial park and gardens.

16th. Between Argenton and St Benoit lies a forest that separates Berry from La Marche which is but a poor country. The country is very hilly, which had been almost a dead flat hill about a league on the other side of Argenton. The Limousin is still a worse country. There grows no wheat in it and it produces very little wine. The peasants live very much on chestnuts which are in great plenty. They have enclosures of dry stone walls about three feet high. They pay no duty upon salt, nor upon imported wines, all over the Limousin. I lay at Limoges.

17th. Limoges is an ugly town. The streets are narrow and the houses built with wood. There are old walls still round it. There are several convents in the suburbs. The Benedictine's garden is very pretty. The government of Limousin is worth upwards of forty thousand livres a year. The Duke of Berwick,[48] the present Governor has never been here.

18th. There is a presidial at Limoges. It depends upon the parliament of Bordeaux.

19th. What they call the city is without the walls of the town. The jurisdiction of it depends entirely on the Bishop. The Cathedral, which they say was built by the English, is in the city. It is not finished. The suburbs of Limoges lie all round the town and are very large. The river that runs near the town is not navigable. There is a handsome bridge over it.

20th. There are a good many vineyards about the town of Limoges and along the river which has two bridges over it, both near the town. I lodged at the Three Kings. The orders to be observed in the cathedral are placed in the choir with this title: *The Dean and chapter of the church of Limoges, which is in no way subject to the church of Rome etc.*

21st. My chaise was mended and I left Limoges. At the third post the roads grew so narrow, and the horses were so little used to draw, that I was obliged to fasten the chaise to a cart drawn by oxen. They draw entirely by the horns. Their heads are fasten'd pretty near one another and half of each horn that joins the other is cut off. I got on horseback and lay at Cercles, a little village. Perigort is not much better country than the Limousin. There is more wine and corn in it, but the face of the country is pretty much the same.

22nd. The only town I pass'd between Limoges and Bordeaux was Libourne. It is surrounded by old walls and is situated on the Dordonne which throws itself into the Garonne below Bordeaux. There come a great many Dutch ships at this season to Libourne where they take in the Bergerac white wine which is sweet. I came to Bordeaux in the afternoon.

23rd. There are two fairs here, one in March and the other in October. Each last thirteen days. There is some trifling abatement made in the customs during these times.

---

48 The Duke of Berwick was the son of James II and Arabella Churchill, sister of the Duke of Marlborough. He fled England during the Revolution and fought for King James in Ireland, then in Flanders, becoming a marshal of France in 1706. In 1707 he effectively established Philip V as king of Spain by his decisive victory at Almansa.

24th. Chateau Trompette is an oblong square so that it has six bastions. It is built with hewn stone.

25th. The Carthusian convent has a fine enclosure belonging to it. The Jacobins are building their convent very handsomely.

26th. The two or three first leagues from Bordeaux the country is covered with vineyards, but then the lands, as they call them begin; which is the most dismal desart country I have seen. There is hardly a tree to be seen for twenty leagues and then one sees nothing but fir trees for the soil is the same till within a league of Bayonne. There is nothing like a town and the villages are made up of a few scattered houses, and even such villages are scarce. All the firs are stripped of their (foliage) every year.

27th. Near Bayonne I observed a tree they call Liège[49] that bears an acorn something like an oak. They fatten their hogs with it which are famous in this country. I got to Bayonne and lodg'd at the St Etienne.

28th. There are two rivers run thro' Bayonne. They meet almost in the middle of the town. The town is generally ill-built. There are some houses on the side of one of the rivers that are pretty good. The Cathedral is a large Gothic building. The convents have nothing extraordinary in them.

30th. The bar is about a league and a half distant from the town. It is very dangerous and ships are frequently lost there. This town subsists chiefly by its trade with Spain.

31st. The Dowager Queen of Spain lives at a half a mile's distance from the town in a very indifferent house. She has built a handsome house not far from it, but has never lived there.

Limoges – M. de Leziers.

Bourdeaux – M. Ainslie, Hyerette, Coughlan.

Bayonne – M. Dadoncourt, Lieut. du Roy. M. Pinsun, Govnr. de la citadelle. Mr Domar. M. St Mar La Croix. Mr Naigle. La Fitte. Duclos – du Regiment de Dauphine. Mr de Rouse. M. Gorget. M Mahot.

NOVEMBER

1st. The Citadel[50] is separated from the town by the river. It stands upon the hill that commands the town. Bayonne never woul'd admit a garrison, but M.

---

49 A cork oak called Chêne-Liège. An old cork oak can still be seen at Tollymore, Co Down.

50 The citadel at Bayonne, the main gateway to and from Spain, was constructed by Marechal Vauban. He conducted fifty successful sieges, designed over 160 fortresses (including Cambrai and Valenciennes which Lord Limerick would have seen earlier) and never suffered a reverse. His banned treatise on finance, *Dine Royal* (1707), anticipated the events that overwhelmed the French monarchy eighty years later.

Louvois,[51] under the pretence of passing troops, seiz'd the gates of the town and then built the citadel. The townspeople have still some guards about the town.

2nd. I went up Adour which is the largest of the two rivers that run through Bayonne, the other is called the Nivelle. One of the banks of the Adour is cover'd with vineyards. The other bank, at least as far as I went, is flat so there are no vines upon it.

3rd. The bar of Bayonne is very dangerous. It is a narrow passage between two beds of sand. There are few or no English ships come here, but a great many Dutch. They bring chiefly spices, and carry back wine, brandy, (and) chestnuts. They carry on a great trade of whale fishing at St John de Luz which is a port three leagues distant from Bayonne.

4th. There are four bridges at Bayonne, one over the Adour and three over the other river which is not called the Nivelle[52] – I did not meet with any body (who) could tell me the name of it. The Nivelle falls into the sea at St John de Luz. Bayonne is free from all taxes. The women all wear mantles which they use sometimes as veils. There is but one gentleman's family in the town. Their bar was once entirely stopp'd up, and they attribute the opening of it to a St. Leon – I think – who was beheaded near the town. This place has a great trade with Spain when the passages (are) open.

5th. My servant was pretty well recovered and I left Bayonne and lay at Aynhoa a small village four leagues from it. The road lies very much up hill and down hill. I gave nine pistoles[53] to the Spanish officer to pass without performing quarentain. The church of Aynhoa has a double gallery round it. The steeple is neat and built with hewn stone. The houses are built with wood and cover'd with tiles.

6th. About half a mile from Aynhoa runs a rivulet that separates France from Spain. There is now a wooden house over it cover'd with a tent. The posts that support the house are on each bank. The Governor of Bayonne and a Spanish officer meet there to settle the limits of Spain and France (and) to prevent disputes between the peasants of each side which have been very frequent of late, (and) not without bloodshed. Soon after I was got into Navarre I observ'd the ground begin to rise and we were soon got into the Pyrenees.

The mountains are steep, but I went by few precipices. The mountains are not so high as the Alps and have now no snow on them. The valleys are full of

51 The Marquis de Louvois, an evil genius, was Louis XIV's war minister. He reorganised the French army (Martinet was his chief assistant). He was active in the persecution of Protestants after the revocation of the Edict of Nantes. He was unscrupulous but consistent in his aims for the aggrandisement of France.

52 The River Vive flows through Bayonne where it joins the Adour.

53 A pistole was a gold coin equivalent to sixteen English shillings of the time.

little villages. I believe they produce no wheat; most of their bread is made of what the French call millet. They are very lazy. Tho' their valleys are full of little rivers there is no fish to be got but what they have from the sea. Their oxen draw by the horns. I observ'd some carriages without any wheels to them.

I was stopped at Maya, which is a village three leagues from Aynhoa, to have my passport and my goods examin'd. The first that examin'd my pass was an officer who, after he had seen it, sent me word that he must have four reals – about two shillings. The next was a custom house officer who examin'd my things slightly, in hopes of a reward. I was afterwards stopp'd by people that call'd themselves the Governor's Guards and was forced to give them at the rate of a shilling a head for me and my servants. I dined at Lizonde, a village about a league from Maya and lay at (omitted by LL) two leagues further.

The houses I have seen in Spain are built (of) stone; several of them with hewn stone of a reddish colour. Those that are anything tolerable are large, the front mostly upon porticos and iron balconys to the first storey, but no glass to their windows. They speak little else but Basque here. Their lights are lamps with oyl. My bedchamber looks like a chandler's shop, but it is hung with millet instead of candles.

There hangs an inscription before an image in the church that promises forty days indulgence in the Bishop of Pamplona's name to all that say a salve before it.

7th. I left Beronetta at six in the morning and did not get to Pamplona till four in the afternoon. The distance is about seven leagues. From Beronetta to Lans, which is three leagues, I was constantly going up and down a steep mountain; but afterwards the road is pretty even. There are mountains on each side which grow less and less as they draw near to Pamplona, which is the capital of Navarre. It stands on a rising ground in the middle of a plain surrounded with mountains, some at half a league and some at a league's distance. The town is built chiefly with brick, which I observe they use flatways. The houses are tiled and the roof hangs over the wall. The balconys have lattices upon their rails. There is very little glass in the windows.

The place is large; one side of it is taken up with a nunnery. There is a large space between the town and the citadel that is planted. The two bastions that look towards the town are upon a level with the place, but the rest of the citadel is much lower than the town. There is nothing extraordinary in the cathedral. What they shew'd me for the palace of the Kings of Navarre is very indifferent. I saw a great many here dressed with the cloak and band. There are three parish churches, besides the cathedral, and nine or ten convents in Pamplona.

8th. I left Pamplona. For two leagues and a half I hardly saw a tree, then I came thro' a wood of evergreen oaks. They are shap'd pretty much like another oak. I did not see any high ones among them. Their leaf is of a very deep green. There are little woods of them, with some intervals, for a league and a half. The road lies thro' a valley with high hills on each side. Then I pass'd a village that stands on a rising ground and then came down into another valley that brought me two leagues farther to Tafalla.

The hills are barren. The valleys produce a good deal of corn, but I saw few vineyards and no olives till I drew near Tafalla which is a pretty little town on the side of a hill. Just without the town there is a handsome chappel that belongs to a nunnery. It has a cupola; the altarpieces are of wood with figures and flowers indifferently wrought. There is a bridge with three large arches just by the town that has not a drop of water under it now. I suppose there come down torrents from the mountains sometimes. Both here and at Pamplona they keep their water in great earthen pots. They complain much of drought this year.

9th. From Tafalla to Marsilia is four leagues over a desart plain till within half a mile of Marsilia where there is a good deal of corn and some olives. There are some hedge rows about the village. From Marsilia to Valtierra is three leagues over a desart plain. About half a mile on this side of Marsilia I cross'd the river Arragon. I observ'd a ferry boat there which I suppose they are oblig'd to use when floods come down. About half a league beyond Valtierra I cross'd the Ebro in a boat and lay at a single (storey) house near the river.

10th. I dined at Sanbronigo three leagues from the Ebro. The road to it lies upon a flat (plain) not much cultivated till within a mile of the town. There are several groves of olives about it. It is the last town in Navarre. About half a league from it I got into the mountains that separate Castille, Arragon and Navarre. I did not go up any of the mountains, but kept in the valleys that run between them for about four leagues. I lay at Agreda which is about a league further.

I observ'd some of the valleys in Castille well cultivated. They had, most of them, little trenches for water running thro' them; I believe they bring it from the hills. They reckon Agreda a very large town because it has a thousand inhabitants.

11th. I dined at Inojosa three leagues from Agreda. The road lies thro' a valley till within half a league of Inojosa where I cross'd a high hill that is well wooded. From Inojosa to Almaray, where I lay, the road lies thro' a great plain that is more cultivated than any part of Spain I have yet pass'd thro'. I went by Almenar and two or three villages. The view from this plain is terminated by mountains at a great distance.

12th. I dined at Villasays four leagues from Almaray. I pass'd by Almassan which is half way. It stands on the side of a hill and is surrounded by a wall.

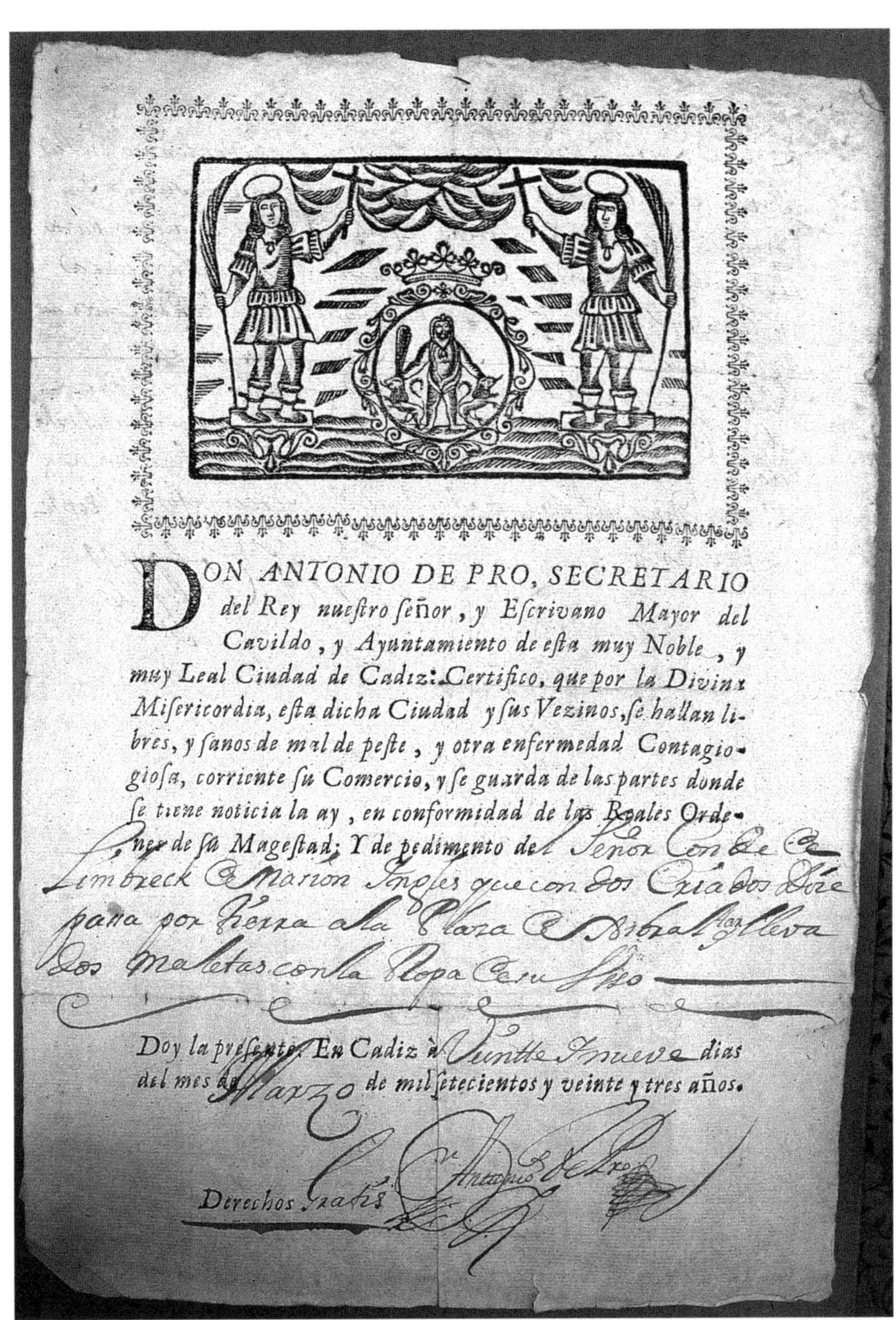

Pass issued in Cadiz, 29th March 1723

El Excell.mo señor Conde de Limerick Contenido en la
Patente de la buelta llegò a esta Ciudad con sus dos
Criados y fueron admitidos a Comercio, y sale aora para
Estepona o Marvella Con la Lancha Real desta plaça
y lleva su Ropa de Vestir, y para que conste donde Convenga
y de estar esta Ciudad su Guarnicion y demas vezinos
Libres y sanos de toda Enfermedad Contagiosa, y guardar
de la Ciudad de Marvella y de todas las partes Sospechosas
doy la presente firmada de my mano en Gibraltar a
Quatro Dias del Mes de Abril de Mil Setecientos y Veinte
y tres años

D. Ths. Crosse.
Lec.

Pass issued in Gibraltar, 4th April 1723

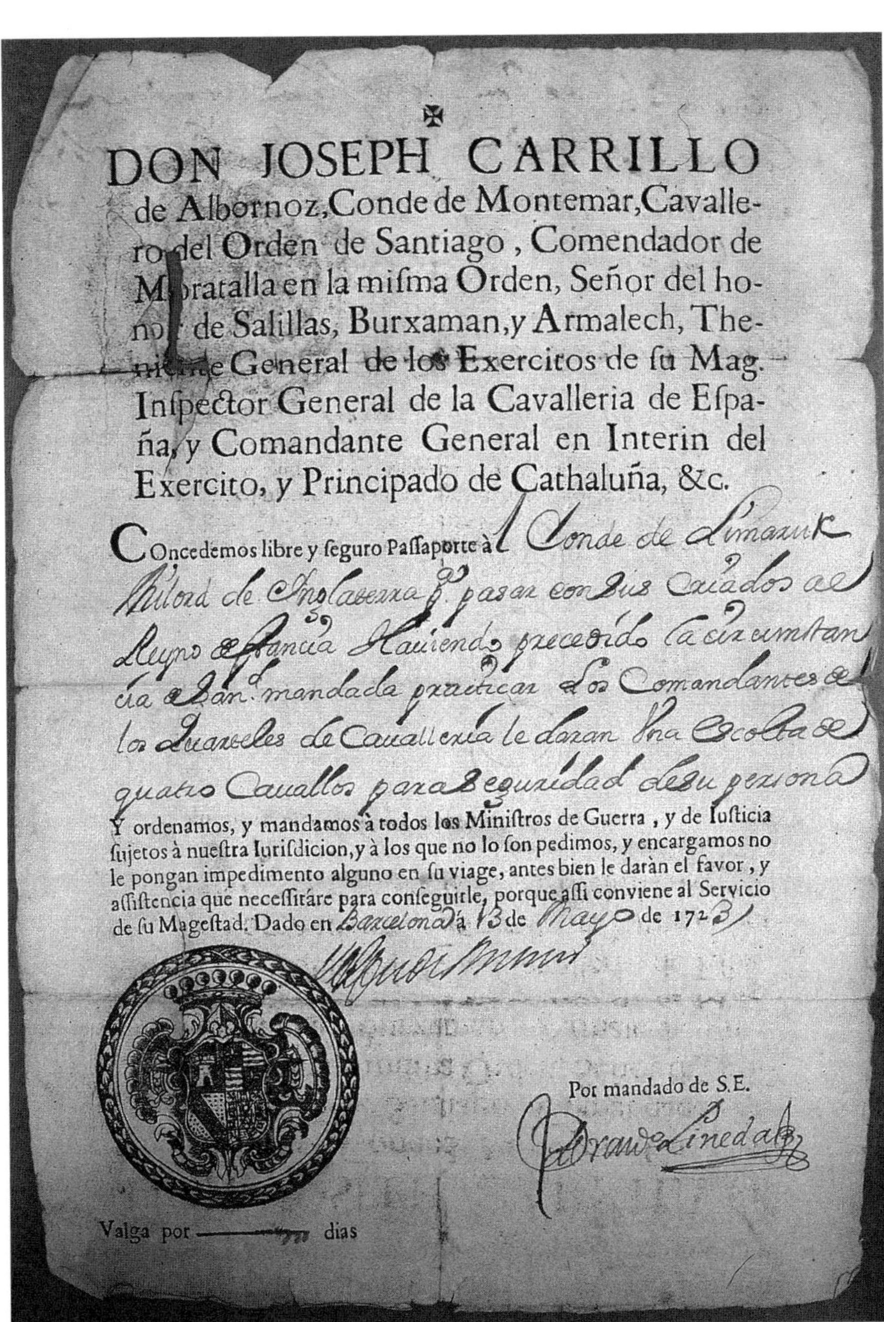

DON JOSEPH CARRILLO

de Albornoz, Conde de Montemar, Cavalle-
ro del Orden de Santiago, Comendador de
Moratalla en la mifma Orden, Señor del ho-
nor de Salillas, Burxaman, y Armalech, The-
niente General de los Exercitos de fu Mag.
Infpector General de la Cavalleria de Efpa-
ña, y Comandante General en Interin del
Exercito, y Principado de Cathaluña, &c.

Concedemos libre y feguro Paffaporte à *Conde de Limaruk
Milord de Inglaterra ā pafar con fus Criados al
Reyno de Francia. Hauiendo precedido la circumtan
cia de San mandada praticar Los Comandantes de
los Quarteles de Caualleria le daran Una Efcolta de
quatro Cauallos para Seguridad de fu perfona*
y ordenamos, y mandamos à todos los Miniftros de Guerra, y de Iufticia
fujetos à nueftra Iurifdicion, y à los que no lo fon pedimos, y encargamos no
le pongan impedimento alguno en fu viage, antes bien le daràn el favor, y
affiftencia que neceffitàre para confeguirle, porque affi conviene al Servicio
de fu Mageftad. Dado en *Barcelona* à *13* de *Mayo* de 172*3*

Por mandado de S.E.

Valga por ———— dias

Pass issued in Barcelona, 13th May 1723

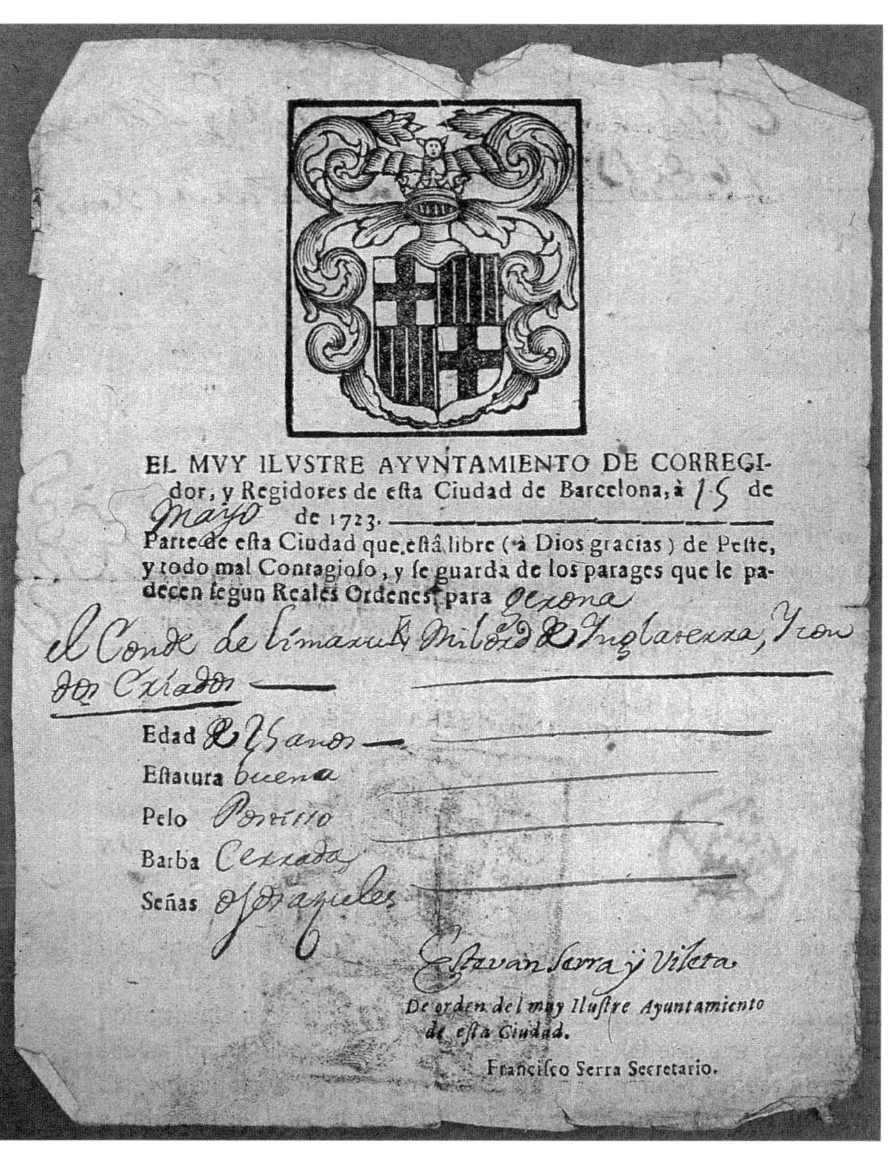

Pass issued in Barcelona, 15th May 1723

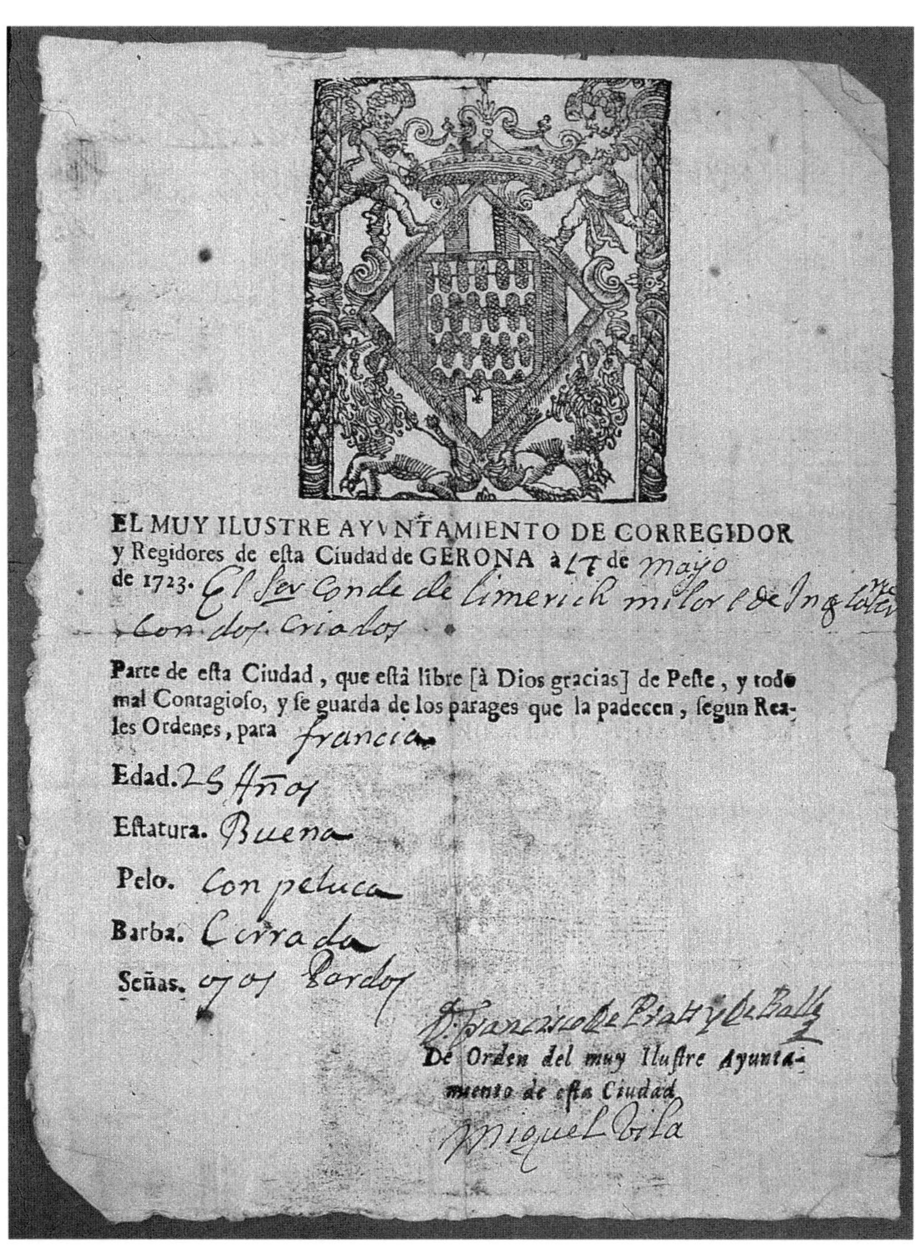

Pass issued in Gerona, 17th May 1723

At Brussels from . (1722)

Mr Jean de Cleves

July	—	—	Receiv'd	50 - 00 - 00
August 31			Receiv'd	50 - 00 - 00
Sep: 19			Receiv'd	50 - 00 - 00

At Paris from Mr Ouchterlony

| Oct: 4 | | Receiv'd | 100 - 0 - 0 |
| Oct: 10 | | Receiv'd | 68 - 0 - 0 |

At Bourdeaux from Mr Ainslie

| Oct: 24 | Receiv'd | 32 - 0 - 0 |

At Madrid from Mr Crean

| Dec: 7 | 150 - 0 - 0 |
| Dec: 28 | 150 - 0 - 0 |

At Lisbon from Mr Goddard

| March. 15. 1723 | 123 - 15 - 0 |

At Barcelona from Mess: Wynder &c.

| May 15 1723 | 50 - 00 - 0 |

Lord Limerick's Financial Transactions

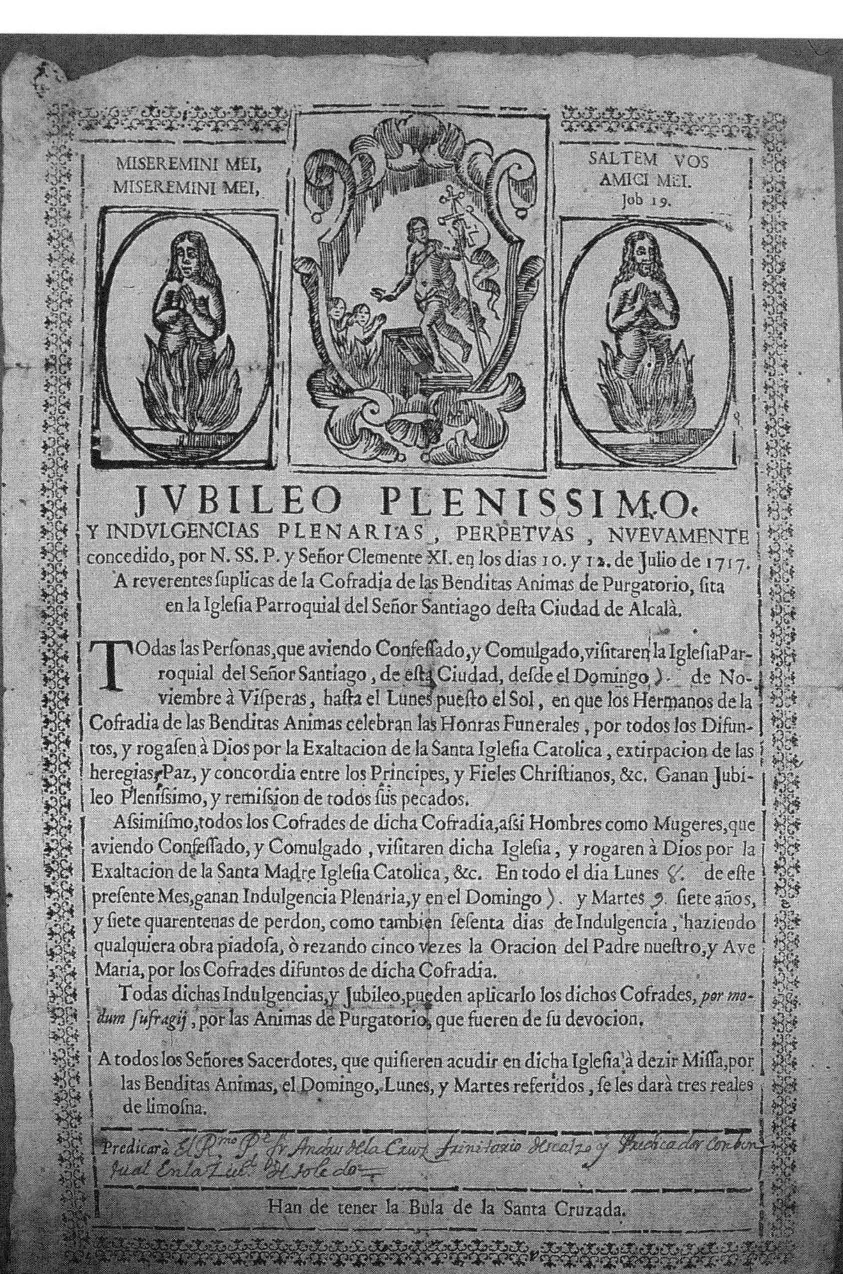

JVBILEO PLENISSIMO.

Y INDVLGENCIAS PLENARIAS, PERPETVAS, NVEVAMENTE

concedido, por N. SS. P. y Señor Clemente XI. en los dias 10. y 12. de Julio de 1717.
A reverentes suplicas de la Cofradia de las Benditas Animas de Purgatorio, sita
en la Iglesia Parroquial del Señor Santiago desta Ciudad de Alcalà.

TOdas las Personas, que aviendo Confessado, y Comulgado, visitaren la Iglesia Parroquial del Señor Santiago, de esta Ciudad, desde el Domingo) de Noviembre à Visperas, hasta el Lunes puesto el Sol, en que los Hermanos de la Cofradia de las Benditas Animas celebran las Honras Funerales, por todos los Difuntos, y rogasen à Dios por la Exaltacion de la Santa Iglesia Catolica, extirpacion de las heregias, Paz, y concordia entre los Principes, y Fieles Christianos, &c. Ganan Jubileo Plenissimo, y remission de todos sus pecados.

Assimismo, todos los Cofrades de dicha Cofradia, assi Hombres como Mugeres, que aviendo Confessado, y Comulgado, visitaren dicha Iglesia, y rogaren à Dios por la Exaltacion de la Santa Madre Iglesia Catolica, &c. En todo el dia Lunes ✠ de este presente Mes, ganan Indulgencia Plenaria, y en el Domingo). y Martes ⒐ siete años, y siete quarentenas de perdon, como tambien sesenta dias de Indulgencia, haziendo qualquiera obra piadosa, ò rezando cinco vezes la Oracion del Padre nuestro, y Ave Maria, por los Cofrades difuntos de dicha Cofradia.

Todas dichas Indulgencias, y Jubileo, pueden aplicarlo los dichos Cofrades, *por modum sufragij*, por las Animas de Purgatorio, que fueren de su devocion.

A todos los Señores Sacerdotes, que quisieren acudir en dicha Iglesia à dezir Missa, por las Benditas Animas, el Domingo, Lunes, y Martes referidos, se les darà tres reales de limosna.

Predicarà el Rmo. Pe. Fr. Andrès de la Cruz, Trinitario Descalzo y Predicador Conbentual en la Ciudad de Toledo

Han de tener la Bula de la Santa Cruzada.

An indulgence of July 1717

The first pasture I have seen for cattle is about Almassan. The grass is almost as short as on the Downs in England, yet there was a number of cattle grazing on it. I lay at Pareres two leagues only from the place I dined at. Half way there is a village that stands very high. The church is built on a rock from whence there is a large prospect, but not a very agreeable one. It is a view of a large plain terminated by mountains at a great distance but not diversified with trees, water or towns.

13th. I came from Pareres to Miraelvio, about seven leagues. The road lies up and down hill most of the way. Miraelvio is an indifferent village, but its church is very pretty within. Its roof is supported by six pillars. It is about ninety foot long and five and forty foot broad. It stands on the brink of a precipice from whence there is an agreeable prospect.

14th. Hita is a small town on the side of a hill about a league from Miraelvio. There are the ruins of a castle on top of the hill. Briknega is about a league and a half from this. The road as far as Hita was hilly. From thence till I pass'd the river Henares – which had very little water in it – the road is mostly upon the descent. As soon as I pass'd the river I found myself in a great plain, bounded on one side by a long ridge of hills with the river running at the bottom of them.

I went about a league from Guadalaxara, a town pleasantly situated on a rising ground between the river and the mountains. As I drew near Alcalá, which has the river between it and the mountains, I observ'd the side of the river that looks towards (the mountains) is planted very thick with trees. The country I came thro' today is pretty well cultivated and peopled, considering it is in Spain. From Mirelvio to Alcalá is nine leagues.

15th. There are eight, or nine and thirty colleges in Alcalá,[54] but they are very small. The Collegio Mayor, which was founded by Cardinal Ximenes is pretty large. The great quadrangle has three rows of piazzas, one above another, of hewn stone. There are besides other little courts, but it is rather what they call in Oxford, the schools, rather than a college, for they told me there were not more then fourteen that eat and lay there. The rest only come to lecture to their several schools. The chappel where the Cardinal is buried is a poor one, and his tomb seems not to be extraordinary. There was a altar rais'd over it for some service that was to be performed so I could not see it distinctly. I observ'd a cardinal's cap on the altar.

The Irish college is a poor building. The foundation is for sixteen and is of eighty years standing. The King's college joins to the Jesuits and is very small. The Jesuits have a handsome church. The cathedral is a poor one. The houses are indifferent.

From Alcalá to Madrid is six leagues. I pass'd over two handsome bridges, one about half way and the other about a league from Madrid but there is

54 Alcalá de Henares, founded in 1510, had been an important university but was subsequently moved to Madrid. It was the birthplace of Cervantes.

hardly any water under them. It is a great plain from Alcalá with some gentle risings. I did not see Madrid till within a league and a half of it. It appears very long and to have a great number of spires, but not high ones.

16th. The streets of Madrid are ill-paved with little pebbles, much like those of London. There are no posts to keep the coaches from those that walk.

The church of Nuestra Senora de Atocha is about half a mile from Madrid. The church is built with brick (while) the door cases of the front and the capitals of the pillars are of stone. The court of the convent that joins to the church is handsome. The cloister is supported with pillars of stone, as is the gallery that runs over it. The church takes its name from an image of the Virgin that is in great veneration here. The image was originally call'd Nuestra Senora de Antiochia but, upon performing a miracle in a bush, her name was changed to de Atocha. The church is filled with pictures of the miracles she has perform'd. It is here the King of Spain hears Te Deum when he has occasion to hear it. There are a great many colours and standards hung up in this church. There is an inscription near the door that says this image was made by St Luke at Antioch and was brought to Spain by some disciples in the lifetime of the Virgin.

The walls near Madrid are many of them built with nothing but mud and the best are a mixture of brick and mud.

18th. There are two theatres where they act Spanish plays. One is call'd the Theatre of the Prince, and the other of the Cross. There is a great cross at the entrance of the last. There comes in light at the top which they shut up when it grows dark and light candles. The pit is pav'd with pebbles. On each side of it there are nine or ten rows of benches, one above another. The amphitheatre is fill'd with nothing but ordinary women. Over that, and over the benches, are balconys for people of fashion.

19th. The great college of the Jesuits has a very handsome church belonging to it. The front of it is stone which is a rarity here. The horse market is kept every Thursday in the Prado.[55]

20th. The Buen Retiro is separated from the town by the Prado. There is a convent joining to it that has two handsome quadrangles. The church is full of guilding, as indeed are all the churches in Madrid. There is an image of the Virgin in it finely adorned with jewels.

21st. There is hardly such a thing as a pair of coach horses in Madrid. The mules which they use to their coaches are very dear. Some of them cost fourscore pistoles. None but Ladies of the first quality go in chairs. The first chairman is generally uncover'd. He that goes behind is supported by two servants.

22nd. There are obsequies performed in the great church of the Jesuits for all

---

55 A wide street where the Prado Museum is now situated. The Buen Retiro is a park laid
    out by Philip IV.

the officers kill'd in the wars. The Jesuit that preach'd made frequent use of this expression – *La antiqua militia Espanola defunta.*

23rd. I walk'd round the town in two hours, tho' in several places I was obliged to go at some distance from the outmost houses because of gardens in some places and of uneven ground in others.

24th. All provisions, especially wine, pay a great tax at coming into Madrid. There is a particular place close to the walls where they kill all their beef and mutton. Tho' Madrid may be said to be wall'd round, it is not at all regular. In some parts the walls of gardens – which are mostly mud – in others the walls of the houses themselves are a kind of wall to the town, for there is no coming into Madrid but thro' gates where there are custom house officers.

25th. There is no such thing as hanging in Spain for any kind of robbing. The galleys for a certain time is their greatest punishment for that crime.

26th. They reckon an hundred & fifty thousand inhabitants in Madrid.

27th. No letters are delivered out at the general post office till the King has read his.

28th. The facade of the Palace is very handsome. Vignola[56] was the architect. It is of stone. The side walls of the great court are stuck full of busts. The entrance into the court is under an arch at one corner.

29th. They are building a handsome bridge over the Mancarares in the road to Toledo. It is of hewn stone, built at the expense of the town, and has nine arches. The Corregidor[57] of Madrid lays a new tax upon meat made use of in the town when such a work is undertaken.

30th. The Prado is two leagues from Madrid. The house is small but prettily situated. The King goes there frequently to shoot.

Dukes of Mirandola, Popoli, Verguas, Medina Celi.
Princes Pio, Celemare, Tachi, Pictorano.
Mons. Marsillac, Comingcour, Cecil, Termini, Lucques, Arsan, La Roche, Le Gendre, Stalpard.
Mr Stratford, Keene, Holzendorf, Blayre, Sample.

DECEMBER

1st. The King of Spain receives a thousand pistoles a day for the duty upon snuff.

2nd. There are three troops of horse guards, one of Spaniards, another of Italians and another of Flemish. There is a regiment of Spanish foot guards as numerous as the Walloon regiment.[58] The regiment of Walloons, consisting of four thousand men, is the only foot guards the King has.

---

56 Giacomo Vignola (1507-1573) was an Italian architect based in Rome.
57 The city governor.
58 The Walloons were from southern Belgium that had been part of the Spanish Empire.

3rd. The military orders of Spain are those of Alcantara, Calatrava and Saint Iago. They have each of them considerable commanderys belonging to them.

4th. When any sum of money is paid, he that receives it gives a chavre – about a third part of a halfpenny – out of each crown.[59]

5th. Their manner of cleaning the streets is with long brushes. Sometimes one sees fifteen of them at work together. They shove the filth down the gutters.

6th. The Ladies here use breast jewels very much. When they are in ceremony their bodys are generally of black velvet, and their petticoats of brocade.

7th. The sallary of a Lady of the Bedchamber to the Queen is eight hundred pistoles a year.

8th. The breast jewel the ladies wear is call'd (a peto).[60] Their husbands make them presents of them before they are married. The jewel is carried by some lady related to the man attended by all his near female relations. And the lady that receives the jewel is attended by her relations.

9th. To be President of Castille one must be (a) Grandee of Spain. But as it seldom happens that the King cares to make any of them president, the business of the place is perform'd by one who has not the title. However, he is generally call'd President of Castille.

10th. Since Catalonia and Arragon were reduced by this King they are not govern'd by a Viceroy but by a Captain General. Navarre is the only province that retains that privilege.

11th. Everything is sold by the pound in Madrid, except butter.

12th. The Venetian ambassador made his entry on horseback, follow'd by the King's coach with four mules but no postillion.

13th. The Genouese envoy made his entry in the King's coach, followed by his own coaches.

14th. I went to Pinto, a village three leagues from Madrid, where the Duke of Ossina gave a bull-feast. I saw six bulls kill'd. They first tir'd them by fixing little darts in their necks and throwing their cloaks in their way. And then they kill'd them with swords.

15th. The Escurial is seven leagues from Madrid. The first four leagues are good road, the rest are hilly and rocky.

16th. The Escurial was built by Philip the Second. The Palace is but a small part of the building. The monks live in the best and most magnificent part of it. The mausoleum is under the great altar. It was finished by Philip the Fourth. Charles the Fifth is the first of the kings buried there. The King's children are buried in another. I believe the convent is the largest in Europe. They reckon fifteen cloisters in it, and two colleges, besides the monks. The Prior is nam'd by the King and is only for three years. The chief front of the

---

59 Possibly the origin of Irish 'luck penny' still current in many livestock transactions.

60 A marriage pendant, or 'peto'. They were usually a triangular, floral-patterned jewel set with diamonds, pearls and precious stones.

convent looks towards the mountain. That and the north front are regular, the other two fronts are not entirely so. The great staircase and the church are mostly painted by Jordano.[61]

17th. From the Escurial to Balsain are eight leagues thro' a desart country. The first three leagues are on a flat but the rest is over one of the steepest mountains I have pass'd. It is (so) deep in snow that my coach could not pass. It is call'd La Sierra de Fuenfria.

18th. Balsain is a little village where the Kings of Spain had a hunting seat. It was burn'd in Charles the Second's time; all except one tower which the King lives in till the Granja is finish'd.[62] It is half a mile distant from Balsain and belonged to the Jeronomites of Segovia from whom the King has bought it. The situation is very agreeable for a summer seat. It is surrounded by mountains on three sides, and before it lies the great plain of Segovia. They have some very fine Spanish marble here that is preparing for the fountains. There will be a great command of water; it comes from the mountains.

Segovia is two leagues from this. It stands partly upon a bottom. It is supplied with water by an acqueduct that brings it from the mountains. It was built by Tragan, or in his time, tho' the inhabitants call it the work of Hercules. It runs even with the ground till it comes to the entrance of the town. Then, as the ground falls, it rises upon arches till it carries the water to the highest part of the town. Great part of it is upon a double row of arches. It is one of the best finish'd and most perfect remains I have seen. There is nothing extraordinary in the cathedral but an indulgence for seventy thousand years for those that pray before a certain image.

19th. The castle stands upon a rock at one end of the town. The ascent to it is impracticable on all sides. It is divided from the town by a ditch that seems to be natural. There are very handsome rooms in it. The ceiling of the King's apartment is entirely gilded. In one room are the statues of the kings – and queens by inheritance – with their names and dates under them. There is a great manufacture of cloth here. The finest sells for a pistole a Spanish yard, which is shorter than ours. From Segovia to Guardarama is six leagues.

20th. From Guardarama to Madrid is nine leagues thro' a poor country. There is a kind of a wall to a kind of park belonging to the Escurial that runs along part of the road.

21st. When an ambassador makes his entry it is upon one of the King's horses.

22nd. The ambassadors here had fifteen hundred pistoles from the King a year in lieu of the freedom of the taxes that are paid at the gates of Madrid.

---

61   Luca Giordano (1634-1705) was the most important Italian decorative artist of his time. He spent ten years working in Spain, including the Escorial.

62   Granja was Philip V's version of Versailles, The highlight of the extensive park and gardens is a series of fountains which reach over fifty feet in height. The palace was again damaged by fire in 1918.

But Cardinal Alberoni[63] took it from them and it is not yet returned.

23rd. The Casa del Campo is at the foot of the descent that comes from the palace but on the other side of the river. There are some water works in the garden with an equestrian statue of Philip the Third. There are several family pictures in the apartment; one of the Emperor Maximilian, Philip, his wife, Charles the Fifth, Ferdinand, & Mary.

24th. One sees nothing this day but presents, going from one to another, of all kinds of eatables.

25th. A company in the Walloon or Spanish Guards is worth about six hundred pistoles a year; and they and the Horse Guards are the only part of the army that is well paid.

26th. The largest and best streets of Madrid have a great many ugly houses mix'd amongst the good ones.[64]

27th. There are five Secretarys of State. The Marquess Grimaldo for forreign affairs, The Marquess de Castelar for war, Don Andreas de Pez for marine affairs and the Indies, The Marquis de Campo Florido for the hazienda.

28th. The Viceroys of Peru and Mexico used formerly to buy their places and had little or no sallary. Now the King gives those employments gratis, and allows them a sallary but not large enough to free them from the necessity of plundering.

29th. I was presented to the King and Queen. They stood at the end of a long room. We made three bows coming in and going out.

30th. The King has restored the privileges of Biscay, which Alberoni took from them, so that they pay little or no duty in any part of Biscay.

31st. The monks of the Escurial are Jeronomites, as are most of the convents adjoining to the King's houses in Spain. It is an order not known in France, and was banish'd (from) Italy because one of the Order attempted to murder St Charles Borrhomeo.

Dona Setaphina de Cordona; alias Dona Antonia Rodrigues.
Dona Matilda Arrao.
Duchess St Pierre, de la Mirandola, de Sulferino, de Arcos, de Popoli, de Livia.
Countess de St Estevan, de Cogolludo.
Marquis Grillo, Mari.
Don Tiberio, & Lelio Caraffa, two Sangris.

---

63 Cardinal Alberoni, while doing his best to restore Spain's economy after the war, alienated most other European capitals. After Philip's failure in Sardinia and Sicily Alberoni was forced to return to Italy.

64 One of the reasons given why people didn't want to build decent houses was because they risked having to house the extensive court retinues that had converged on Madrid.

JANUARY 1723

1st. I was surpris'd with what a gentleman of some rank in the service of Spain told me, that Alberoni was averse to the late war and that it was entirely the King's work who is fond of war, and fancy'd all the troops of France would come over to him

2nd. When the Spaniards made their first descent in the island of St Domingo[65] they compute that there was eight millions of souls in it, and now there is not more than one hundred thousand.

3rd. When Columbus propos'd to Ferdinand, the catholick, to undertake the discovery of the West Indies, he treated the proposal as chimerical. But his wife, Isobel who was queen of Castille in her own right, came into it and supplied Columbus with money and ships. But with this (proviso) that the natives of Arragon – her husband's natural subjects – have no more right to anything in the Indies than foreigners.

4th. Each troop of guards is of two hundred in time of peace. The barracks that are building for them will be able to contain a thousand.

5th. Tho' the facade of the palace was designed by Vignola, it is not executed entirely upon his plan.

6th. The order of Calatrava begun in the year 1156. Calatrava is in the kingdom of New Castile as it was then one of the frontier towns of the christians. It was given to the Knights Templars that they might defend it against the moors who at this time were making great preparations to attack it. The Knights Templars thought themselves unable to defend it, so they deliver'd it up to the King of Castile, Sancho, who had just then succeeded his father, the Emperor Alonso. As no one else offer'd to undertake the defence of it the King gave the town, and country adjoining, to two monks who founded the order of Calatrava. It was confirmed by a bull of Pope Alexander the Third in the year 1164. Don Gracia was the first great master of the order.

7th. The first university that was founded in Spain was at Palentia in the year 1209 by Alonso, King of Castile, grandson to Alonso call'd the Emperor.

8th. In the year 1240, Ferdinand, King of Castile, remov'd the university founded at Palentia by his grandfather to Salamanca.

9th. The Buen Retiro was built in the time of Philip the fourth. There is a great deal of room in it but I did not see one good apartment. There is a statue of the King on horseback in the garden that they value at thirty thousand pistoles. The horse is supported by his hind legs only.

10th. The King of Spain has now twelve or thirteen thousand horse and dragoons in his service.

11th. In time of war there were undertakers that remounted the King of Spain's troops at the rate of fourteen pistoles a horse.

12th. In the year 1175, Don Pero Ferdandez obtain'd a bull from Pope

---

65 St Domingo (and Haiti) was discovered by Columbus in 1492. Within a generation the original natives had been swept aside by the Spaniards.

Alexander for the institution of the order of St Iago. He was the first master of the order. One of their institutions was that thirteen knights should always accompany the master, and once a year shou'd hold a general chapter of the order.

13th. In the year 1214, Alonso, King of Leon, took Alcantara from the moors and, as it lay much expos'd, he gave it to some knights of the order of Calatrava that they might defend it. This was the beginning of the order of Alcantara who, by degrees, exempted themselves from the jurisdiction of the order of Calatrava. Pope Julio the Second granted a bull in their favour.

14th. There are about an hundred battallions of foot now in Spain.

15th. King James of Arragon conquer'd Majorca in the year 1230.

16th. Ferdinand, King of Castile, took Cordona from the moors in the year 1236.

17th. The King of Arragon took Valencia in the year 1238.

18th. Alfonso the tenth, King of Castile, was chosen Emperor in the year 1256 by one part of the electors but he never enjoyed that dignity.

19th. The armoury is near the King's stables. They shew the armour this King was crown'd in. They told us all the Kings of Spain are crowned in armour.

20th. In the sermon P. Frias, a Jesuit, preach'd this day he advanced this doubt; whether Christ did more honour to St Sebastion in making him a visit, or St Sebastion to Christ by receiving him in his house.

21st. The King of Spain has now nine ships of the line of battle, five frigates and six galleys.

22nd. The massacre of the French in Sicily was in the year 1283, at Easter.

23rd. In the year 1096, Urban the Second summon'd a council to meet at Clermont in Auvergne in order to undertake the holy war. And in the year 1291 Elpis, King of Egypt, took Ptolemais from the christians, which was the last town that remain'd of all the christian conquests.

24th. The greatest part of the King of Spain's revenues in the West Indies arise from the duty every thing that comes in, or goes out, pays. They hardly work any mines for the King's account.

25th. The Jesuits extoll the parts and learning of the Emperor of China and say the only thing that prevents his turning christian is having but one wife, which he says is no precept of the gospel.

26th. Aranjues is seven leagues from Madrid. The road is good and lies on a flat (plain) all the way.

27th. The house at Aranjues is small and irregular. The gardens are join'd to it by a bridge. They are situated in an island in the Tagus. The walks are narrow and calculated for coolness. They are most of them cover'd walks. There are some noble walks of the island, but none of them answer directly to the house.

28th. Toledo is six leagues from Aranjues. The road lies along the side of the Tagus which runs round the town and gives it the shape of a horseshoe so there is but one way of coming at the town. And the ascent on that side is so steep that it might easily be made very strong.

29th. The great church of Toledo is a gothick building. The riches of it are very great. There is a chappel in it founded by Cardinal Ximenes where the Mocearabick[66] service is performed. It differs very much from the Roman service, particularly in not praying to saints. The palace is situated in the highest part of the town and was a handsome building. It was built, or repaired, by Charles the Fifth. It was burnt in the last war by General Hamilton who commanded the troops of the Emperor there.[67] There are also two bridges over the Tagus. There is a handsome hospital in the plain, without the town, founded by one of the Archbishops of Toledo. In the nuestros de los reyes[68] there are some remains of a moorish palace. The bishop's palace is a large irregular building. The palace of Ferdinand and Isabel is turn'd into a convent. The canons of the cathedral have a particular dress with a long train.

30th. Toledo to Madrid is twelve leagues. The villages I pass'd thro' have nothing remarkable in them.

31st. The first jubilee celebrated in Rome was in the year 1300. That ceremony was instituted by Pope Boniface the Eighth and was to (be) celebrated but once in an hundred years, but Clement the sixth reduced it to fifty, and Sixtus the Fourth to five and twenty years as it now remains.

Le Grand prieur d'Orleans. Le Chevalier de Cri.
Duke of Arcos, of Sulferino, of Bournonville.
Marquis of Risbourg
Don Andreas Afflitto, Goncale Packego y Padillas.

FEBRUARY

1st. In the year 1302, there was held a council of the bishops and prelates of the province of Toledo at Penafiel in Old Castile. The third canon of that council orders that no priest shall keep concubines publickly.

2nd. I supp'd at the Prince of Cellamare's with the Grand Prior.

3rd. The sallary for secretary of state here is two thousand pistoles.

4th. The sallary of the master of the horse is but six hundred.

5th. A gentleman of the bedchamber has an hundred & fifty pistoles a year.

6th. In each troop of guards there is a captain, two lieutenants, an ensign (and) nine exempts.

66 The Mozarabic rite is an ancient liturgy of Visigothic Spain which survived the Moorish suzerainty. It is written in a peculiar dialect of degraded Latin but, with Cardinal Ximenes' support and a certain amount of input, it survived in Toledo.

67 The Emperor, as Archduke Charles, supported by the Allies, had been Philip's rival for the crown of Spain until he succeeded his brother.

68 Possibly San Juan de los Reyes. Originally a Franciscan convent it was turned into a church.

7th. When there is a ball at court the ladies of the bedchamber sit on a bench placed against the wall and the camaristas sit upon the ground.[69]

8th. When there is a play at court all the ladies sit on the ground and the men stand.

9th. The Jesuits of Spain have much more liberty than those of France or Italy.

10th. Ladies of the first quality, when they are presented to the King, kiss his hand.

11th. When the King or Queen pass nobody bows to them.

12th. Five leagues from Madrid I cross'd the Guardarama. It is very low, tho' it frequently overflows. The country is very bare till I came near Allala where there are great plantations of olives. I lay at Albravo, fifteen leagues from Madrid.

13th. About three leagues from Albravo I pass'd the Albericke on a long wooden bridge. A league further is Talevera. A tolerable good town, it was the ancient Ebora. It is now famous for earthen ware which they send all over Spain. Six leagues from thence is Oropesa, a little town prettily situated on a rising ground. I lay at Almaraz eighteen leagues from Albravo.

14th. About half a league from Almaraz is a fine bridge of two arches over the Tagus. It was built by the town of Pazencia. As soon as I pass'd it I got into the mountains which lasted about three leagues till I came to Taraisejo. Three leagues farther is Truzillo. The Turris Julia of the Romans, the town stands in a bottom at the foot of the castle. There are some small remains of antiquity without the town. I lay at Miaijados, a small village fourteen leagues from Almaraz.

15th. Four leagues from Miaijados I cross'd the Guadiana to change horses at Medellin, where there is an old castle. From thence to Merida. I cross'd a fine plain of three leagues. Merida was built by the Romans and call'd Emerita Augusti. There are the remains of two noble acqueducts. The water that furnishes the town comes by a modern acqueduct. The governor told me there was a pillar a league from the town that in the time of the Romans was in the middle of it. The bridge is antique and a very noble one. I lay at Talaveruela, a village fourteen leagues from Miaijados.

16th. From Talaveruela to Badajos is three leagues. The town is not very strong towards the side of Spain. On the other side, of Portugal, it is defended by the river Guadiana which is large and has a handsome bridge over it. There are one or two forts on the rising grounds near the town. It was formerly call'd Pax Augusti, but I could hear of no remains of Antiquity.

At a league from Badajos, Spain is separated from Portugal by a little river called Caya. Two leagues further Elvas stands upon a rising, uneven ground. It is strongly fortified with Ravelines,[70] horn-works and other out-works and,

---

69 Court pages or attendants.

70 A raveline is an external fortification where two walls form a salient angle into which the defender hopes to force the opposition.

besides, it stands on very rocky ground. There is a fort a little distance from the town to which there are two communications underground. There is a cistern in the town which, as the Governour told me, cou'd contain water enough for ten thousand men for six months. He is now finishing an arsenal where he said he would put arms for sixty batallions. I lay at Elvas this night. The acqueduct seems to me not to be of the Romans.

17th. The country about Elvas is full of olives. The first orange and lemon trees I saw grow commonly in gardens (were) there. Six leagues from Elvas I pass'd thro' Estremos, a fortified town, and lay the night at Montemor fifteen leagues from Elvas. The country is hilly and does not seem to afford much corn.

18th. I lay at Aldegaloga, twelve leagues from Montemor. The last five leagues are all upon a deep sand, the other seven lie thro' a country flatter and more plentifull than the day before. This village is situated on the side of the Tagus three leagues from Lisbon.

19th. I was forced to wait till twelve a clock till the tide came in, and had so little wind that I was four hours crossing to Lisbon. The prospect of the town is very beautifull from the water. It stands on a steep ascent from the water.

20th. The mouth of the river of Lisbon is about four leagues from the town.

21st. They reckon upwards of three hundred thousand inhabitants in Lisbon.

22nd. They say the town stands on seven hills. the streets are narrow and the ascents so very steep that unless the middle of the streets were pav'd with brick, it would not be possible for the mules to draw up them. The brick is turn'd edgeways.

23rd. The Palace in Lisbon was built by Philip the Fourth of Spain when this country belong'd to him.

24th. The ground laid out for a palace lies south of the town and has a beautiful prospect of the mouth of the river.

25th. The English college here has about twenty belonging to it.

26th. The Irish college and the Irish nunnery at Belleim[71] were founded by an Irish priest who was confessor to the Dutchess of Bragance, afterwards Queen of Portugal.

27th. The country about Lisbon is very beautifull; full of little country houses with olive and orange trees planted round them.

28th. There are processions every Friday in Lent where there are a number of penitents (who) march (by) whipping themselves. I saw one dragging a heavy chain fasten'd to one leg.

El Marques D'angesus, El Conde D'asumar, Le Marquis de Lannoi, Monsieur Montagnac Consul de France.

Mr Goddard, Marman, Revel, Longville, Bristol, Cevecot, Cross.

L'd Vere, Capt. Clinton, Medley, Wyndham.

71 Belem, on the outskirts of Lisbon, was the launch pad for Portugal's Age of Discoveries and a centre for learning.

MARCH

1st. The few men of war that the King of Portugal has are in wretched order.

2nd. There is but one Secretary of State and his allowance is very inconsiderable.

3rd. Most of the titles in this country are personal, very few are hereditary.

4th. I lay at a gentleman's quinta[72] about five miles from Lisbon. It is near a pretty village call'd Lumiare.

5th. I lay at Mafra about four leagues farther at the Viscount de Puente Lima's. There is a very pretty wood of evergreens near his house cut into walks. The King is now building a church there, and intends adding a palace and convent to it. The church is built with a coarse grain'd marble.[73]

6th. The country about Mafra is very wild and seems barren, but the valleys I saw in returning to Lisbon are very beautifull; full of corn and olives.

7th. Since making a Patriarch, the King had divided Lisbon into two sees and has made his own chappel a Patriarchal one. There is a throne rais'd in the middle of it for the Patriarch.

8th. There are twenty four cannons belonging to the Patriarchal chappel. They are all of good familys and have five hundred pound a year sallary.

9th. The King of Portugal has ten or twelve men in pay. He has no horse guard.

10th. All the English merchants at Lisbon are factors. They have ten percent allow'd them.

11th. One of the Bresil fleets, which they call del Rio, came in this day. There are generally three come from Bresil every year. They take their denomination from the different parts of that country that they come from. This is reckon'd the richest in gold.

I saw the convent of Hieronomites at Belein, which is a very handsome one, tho' it is but half finish'd. The dormitory is the longest I have seen. Several of the kings are buried in the church in kind of marble coffins. One of the inscriptions says, It is said King Sebastion is buried here.

12th. This fleet is said to bring two hundred thousand pound in gold, either coined or un-coined, for the King; and about six hundred thousand for particular people. That is what is registered. There is generally besides a considerable sum that they venture the running of.

13th. I went to see the nunnery at Oclivellas. They are reckon'd about three hundred. They have a great deal of liberty. They are allow'd to keep as many servants as they please and seldom eat in the refectory. Most of them have lovers, and they frequently dine with company at the grate.

---

72 A quinta is a Portuguese estate.

73 The massive monastery-palace at Mafra was begun in 1717 funded by Brazilian gold. No expense was spared and up to 45,000 workers were employed. It all helped to destroy the Portuguese economy and the palace was only used briefly before the royal family fled to Brazil in 1799, taking most of the contents with them.

14th. The convent of St Vincent stands upon a hill at one end of the town. It is a very noble one but it is not quite finish'd. The late King John, who was before the Duke of Braganza, is buried behind the great altar. The chappel of the old cathedral is handsome enough. It is very much gilt. The old castle stands high and commands almost an entire prospect of the town, but it is of no manner of strength.

15th. I cross'd the water and lay at Aldegallega. It is three leagues from Lisbon, yet in clear weather one sees the town and distinguishes the convent of St Vincent very plainly.

16th. I din'd at Agnas de Moro five leagues from Aldegallega. The road lies thro' a large wood of firs. The soil is deep sand. I lay at Porto Caravallo, a single house two leagues farther.

17th. I din'd at Alcacevas, five leagues from where I had lain, and lay at Villa Nova two leagues farther. The country is very barren and neither feeds nor produces anything but just about (enough for) the villages which are small and few. I saw Elbora at a distance. It lies about five leagues from Alcacevas on a rising ground. It is the second university of Portugal. Coimbra is the first. A priest told me there were thirty convents, churches and colleges there.

18th. I came eight leagues to Serpa, the frontier town of Portugal on this side. The country is better towards the frontiers, and has more people. We left the the town of Beja two leagues on the right. I forded over the Quadiana about a league before I came to Serpa. The town has some old walls about it.

19th. I came from Serpa to Puymogo, six leagues, thro' a very mountainous, barren country. The first five leagues are in Portugal, which is separated from Andaluzia by the river Chanza which is not fordable where I pass'd it. Puymogo lies a league from it. There are about two hundred familys there. There is a fort that commands the village. It is a square regularly fortified, with a church in the middle of it. It is now garrison'd by a company of foot.

20th. From Puymogo I came to Alosna; five leagues thro' wretched country that produces neither corn, wine nor oil. Alosna has about three hundred familys in it. An inhabitant in the town told me they did not kill a sheep in the year and yet they have two parsons with ten ecclesiastical assistants.

21st. From Alosna to Veas is six leagues. The country continues still bad till I came near Veas. I came in the evening about half a league further and left Niebla about half a league on the right. The country begins to mend (and) there is a good deal of corn and wine about Villa Rasa.

22nd. Villa Rasa is ten leagues from Sevil. The country is very fruitful and agreeable, and full of villages. The lower grounds are cover'd with corn, and the upper ones with vines and olives. I observ'd they plow under the olive trees. I saw the ruins of a moorish town upon the left. They call it Texada. There is now not one house in it, tho' it was a considerable town in the moor's time. I pass'd within a league of Olivares. I did not see Sevil until I was within half a league of it. The town is situated upon a dead flat and is stretch'd out a great way in length by the banks of the Gaudelquivir. From Lisbon to Sevil is fifty two leagues, besides the passage of the Tagus.

23rd. The cathedral of Seville is a fine gothick building. There are several more modern buildings added to it that make it not regular on the outside. (It has) a sacristy, a large parish church etc. All round these buildings there is a walk with four or five steps up to it and, at certain distances, there are old pillars of several marbles fix'd in the steps. All that get within those pillars enjoy the same privileges as if they were in the church. These pillars were certainly belonging to some Roman building, as well as those round the (ex)change; and many of those made use of in the convents seem to be so too.

I heard the passion sung in the cathedral, where one priest represents our saviour, another Pilate etc. Behind the cathedral stands the exchange, a very handsome, regular stone building. But since the trade of the Indies has been remov'd to Cadiz there is no use made of it.

The Alcácar, which was the moorish palace, makes no appearance on the outside but it is very large and has good rooms in it particularly (one) that is very high. The ceiling in it is well wrought and gilt.

The gardens are very pretty. One particularly has several terraces across it and in the void spaces there are orange and lemon trees so that one may gather them from the terraces. The terraces are supported by arches and under one of them is a bath.

The Hospital of the Charity is a very pretty building. There are two long rooms full of old decrepid people. There is (a) little room (set) apart for the consumptive. It is kept very neat. There is besides a very large hall where as many poor as come are fed every evening.

The convent of Cordeliers is a very noble one. It has two very large cloisters besides several small ones. There is a double corridor round each cloister. There are sometimes two hundred fathers in this convent.

24th. I went about a league from Sevil to see the remains of Italica, for Sevil was originally call'd Hispalis and, afterwards, by Caesar nam'd Julia Romula.[74] Italica was situated on a rising ground near the Guadelvuivir. The only remains are of an amphitheatre, which has been pretty large, and of a place they call Palacios, which looks like a long gallery.

Just without Sevil stands a handsome convent of Carthusians.[75] The cloisters are very neat. There is a chappel with the tombs of an ancestor of the Dukes of Alcalá and his wife that are wonderfully well wrought. The Sacrario behind the great altar is very neat and rich. There is a wooden figure of St Bruno in a little chappel extremely well done. This convent had formerly a

---

74 Founded by Scipio, Italica was one of the earliest Roman settlements in Spain. It was the birthplace of such Roman emperors and generals as Hadrian, Trajan and Theodosius.

75 The fourteenth-century Carthusian monastery is at La Cartuja, extensively restored as part of Expo 1992.

fine breed of horses, but one of the fathers told me that as they had no vent for them of late they had left off breeding.

In the suburb call'd Triana there is a great manufacture of earthen ware. They take the earth for it out of the Guadelquivir. But the very large ones, which they call Tinajos, are made about a league from Sevil. They mix a good deal of sand with the earth.

At the gate of Carmona there is an acqueduct that still furnishes the town with water, near which there is a noble old palace of the Dukes of Alcalá which now belongs to the Duke of Medina Celi. There is a fine room but indifferently furnish'd with books. There is a closet with manuscripts that they call, *libros vedados*. There are two fine statues of a Bacchus and a Hercules and some good busts.

25th. At one end of the Alamada, which is a walk planted with trees, are two handsome (columns) with each of them a figure at the top. The one of Hercules, who they pretend was the founder of this city, the other of Julius Caesar who was the restorer of it. They were put up in Philip the Second's time. The Hospital de la Sangre is without the gates of the town. It seems to be a square building and has thirty five windows in front. It has a handsome church. The Giralda is an hundred and fifty four Varas in height; each Vara is four palms.[76] The prospect from it is very beautifull. The town seems to be about as large as Madrid.

In the afternoon there were several processions and numbers of penitents, some whipping themselves and others carrying crosses. At the nunnery of the Madre de Dios there were several penitents that stood with a naked sword under each arm. The monument in the cathedral was very magnificent. It is a building of three floors. In the first there are twenty pillars, in the second twelve and in the third, I think, nine. At the top is the figure of our Saviour on the cross between the Thieves. It is perfectly well lit with candles and lamps. The custodia is of silver and they say it is twenty hundred weight. I observ'd all the gentlemen of Sevil were in their best cloaths. This is the night of adventures for the women are allowed to run all night from one church to another.

26th. I left Sevil early. The first four leagues are thro' a tolerable good country for pasturage, and pretty flat. And from the Venta at the end of the four leagues to Lebrixa, six leagues more, it is continued plain that in some places seems to be four or five leagues in breadth. It is some of the best pasturage in Spain. There are numbers of cattle of all kinds feeding on it. It is bounded on one side by the Guadelquivir, formerly Betis, and on the other the prospect is terminated by high mountains.

From Lebrixa to Xeres are five leagues. From thence comes the wine we call sherry in England. Puerto de Sta Maria, where I lay that night, is two leagues further.

76 The Giralda, named after the giraldillo, a weather vane on its summit, is part of Seville cathedral.

27th. The wind was so high no boat woul'd pass to Cadiz so I went to see the convent of the Carthusians near Xeres. It is situated just by the Guadalete which was the Lethe of the ancients. The valleys near the river are full of orange trees, and the upper grounds are planted with olives. The convent was famous for breeding good horses but their breed is quite spoilt. The Sagravio behind the great altar is neat and the cloisters are handsome. There are several antient marble pillars there.

28th. From the puerto I came to Cadiz in an hour; it is two leagues across the bay and by land it is eight leagues round. Cadiz stands on one point of the bay and the little town of Rota on the other. Rota is two leagues from the puerto so that in all the bay is ten leagues round.

Tho' the town of Cadiz stands upon little ground yet they say there are upwards of an hundred thousand inhabitants in it. The streets are indeed very narrow and the houses high, and there is hardly a garden in the town except that of the Capucines. The walls of the town stand so near the water that the waves dash against them on every side (except) where the bay is separated from the ocean by a very narrow neck of land which is perfectly well fortified.

There are no remains of antiquity but marble pillars which are scatter'd about in the houses. Most houses that are tolerably good have towers to them.

29th. I read an inscription over a door in Cadiz that the master of the house had upon some occasion receiv'd the host into his house tho', like the centurion in the gospel, he own'd he was not worthy of it.

30th. Three leagues from Cadiz, I cross'd the water in a boat which separates it from the mainland. It is on that point of land that they say stood the Temple of Hercules. From Cadiz to that place there is nothing but a deep sand. I lay on hurdles in a cottage about twelve leagues from Cadiz. They call the place Taivila. From thence to St Roque is seven leagues.[77] That town has been built since we had Gibraltar. Most of the Spanish inhabitants of the place being settled there. It stands on a hill about a league from Gibraltar.

At Seville: Messrs French & Rice

At Cadiz: Mr Nathaniel Hearne, Mr Black, brother to the Consul.

At St Roque: El Marques de Montreal.

APRIL

1st. I walk'd round the fortifications of Gibraltar which are in very good order. The only way the town is capable of being taken is by sea, for the back of the hill where the French got up is made impracticable.

2nd. I went to Europa Point which is the southern most point of Europe. It is five leagues from thence to the hill of Centa which town one sees very plain

---

77 San Roque was founded by Gibraltarians fleeing the English when Gibraltar was captured in 1704.

with a glass. Near this point there is a large reservoir for water support'd by several arches. It seems rather a building of the Romans than the Moors.

3rd. The weather was so bad I cou'd not cross to Centa as I intended.

4th. The Spaniards call St Roque "El Campo de Gibraltar". There are now about two or three hundred soldiers there. The Marquis of Montreal, who commands them, is a major-general. Their advance guard is about a quarter of a mile from Gibraltar.

5th. The neck of land that comes to Gibraltar is very narrow so that with very little expense it might be made an island. Algezira is opposite to Gibraltar on the other side of the bay, which is about two leagues and a half over.

6th. I went from Gibraltar to Estepona by water, from thence I took horses to Marbella thro' a pleasant country. Near the town grows a good many sugar canes. I lay at the house of Don Alvaro Cordero.

7th. Marbella is a little place with the name of a city. It is about twelve leagues by land from Gibraltar yet one sees the rock very plain, which the ancients call'd Calpe, as well as Abila, which is opposite to it, (and) now call'd Apes Hill.[78] My landlord told me he had sugar for three thousand pistoles by him.

8th. From Marbella to Malaga is nine leagues; most part of the way along the shore. There are Atalayas every half league which they light every night.[79] I left Monda about two leagues on the left. 'Tis thought this was not the ancient Munda, for the valley near it is so small that two such armys as Caesar's and Pompey's could scarce engage there. 'Tis generally thought that Ronda la Vieja was the ancient Munda.

9th. The town of Malaga is large and well inhabited. It has fortifications towards the land but (on) the old moorish wall, towards the sea, there is a small fort which defends the entry of the mole[80] but could not hinder ships from landing men five hundred yards below it. As the road is dangerous in some winds they are running out a new mole to cross the old one so that all ships within that will be very safe. There is a large moorish castle a top of the hill. The passage to it is wall'd in but there is a hill near it that commands it.

That part of the cathedral which is finish'd is handsome and has more light than generally the churches have in Spain.[81] The wooden work of the choir is well done. There are the best kitchen gardens about the town that I have seen in Spain.

10th. From Malaga to Antequerra is seven leagues. The road is exceeding bad. It is not safe riding down the Scarnela of Antequerra.[82] I saw in several places in the mountains good corn and fine vineyards. Antequerra is a large town.

---

78 In ancient mythology Calpe and Abyla are the two Pillars of Hercules.

79 Watchtowers.

80 A mole is an artificial harbour or breakwater.

81 The cathedral is still unfinished, the money having been diverted to help the American War of Independence.

82 Limestone gorges.

About a league from it is the Lover's Rock from whence a christian and a moorish girl flung themselves to avoid being taken by her father who pursued them. I lay at La Rua, four leagues farther thro' flat country of corn and olives; the olive trees are planted among the corn.

11th. Cordova is twelve leagues from La Rua. The country abounds in vines, corn and olives. There are besides regular plantations of evergreen oak. They make corks of their bark. I din'd at La Rambla where I tasted a strong white wine that they said was fifty years old. They sell it a real of Plata the quartillo.[83] Montilla is a league from this place. I lay at Cordova.

12th. The Guardelquivir runs close by Cordova; there is a handsome bridge over it. The cathedral of Cordova was the most famous mosque in Spain. It is supported by rows of little marble pillars which have a beautifull effect. Every walk that is made by those rows of pillars has a particular roof to it. In the middle they have taken away the pillars to make a choir and high altar. The custodium is a handsome piece of work. There is a cloister (that) joins to the church and is supported by the same kind of ancient marble pillars.

From the steeple, which is modern, I had a perfect view of the town. I take it to be about three parts in four as large as Seville. The Alcácar is but an indifferent building. It is now made the tribunal of the inquisition. There is a large garden to it planted with orange & lemon trees, but very much neglected. The Bishop's palace is handsome and has a garden that is kept in better order. There is a fountain in it and the close walls are cover'd by orange & lemon trees.

The King's stables are handsome and have room, as they told me, for an hundred and nine horses. I saw but few there and few of them handsome. They ride the horses in a large court joining the stables. The King's mares are kept two or three leagues from the town. The first rider told me that there were about four hundred mares and seventeen stallions.

The convent of the Augustins is handsome. The plain thro' which the Guadelquivir runs is very beautifull (and) it is full of gardens. The hill on the north side of Cordova has several country houses on the side of it, and is planted with several sorts of trees so that it makes a beautifull prospect of the town. The best horses of Spain are bred at Cordova and are particularly valued for being gentle, so much (so) that they pretend nothing will make them kick.

13th. I left Codova and dined at a little town call'd Castro. It is built on the side of a hill on the top of which there is a moorish castle. Most of the towns in these parts are built so; the moors were fond of placing their castles on the top of hills. I lay at Baena, another town two leagues farther. I met with a violent shower of hail this afternoon. This is a plentifull country of corn. The valleys, thro' which there commonly runs a small river, are beautifull. There are

83 A quartillo was just under half a litre. A Plata (debased) real was roughly the equivalent of 6 pence.

wheels on the sides of the rivers that throw up water for the fields and gardens.

14th. Alcalá la Real is six leagues from Baena. The castle is on the top of a hill and the town below it. Five leagues from thence begins the famous Vega of Grenada which is one of the most beautifull valleys in the world. Three leagues farther is Grenada where I lay this night

15th. The situation of Grenada is very particular for there is no place from whence one can see the whole town. It is built partly between two hills and partly on the outside, if one may call it so, of those hills. The Alhambra, which is the moorish palace, is built upon one of them.[84] The building is irregular, but it is very particular and whimsical. It has several courts. One (in) particular they call the Court of the Lions because of a fountain in the middle supported by lions (of) marble that is very handsome. The walks round the court are supported by beautifull marble pillars, and at each (side) there is a vestibule that advances into the court with pillars of the same kind. Out of this court goes the Hall of the Abencerrages, so call'd because so many of them were murder'd there by the last king of the moors. There is a fountain in the middle of the room and they show the stones stain'd, as they say, with their blood. Opposite to this is the Sala de Las dos Hermanos, so call'd because there are large pieces of marble in the pavement of it. They are about fifteen foot long and seven broad. There are besides several handsome rooms, particularly one noble one where the Moors used to dance. They show a closet where a moorish queen used to dress herself. In one corner of it there is a marble stone with several holes thro' it on which she used to stand while they burnt perfumes under it.

Joining to the Baths there is a room with two bed places in it where the king and queen used to lie down after bathing. That of the queen rises in the middle and sinks at each end. The walls of all the rooms are very curious; there are a thousand different figures wrought upon them. They say that the plaster was work'd up with whites of eggs and that one of the moorish kings kept four thousand hens for that purpose. The Marquis de Salar told me that in this country they reckon'd three women for one man.

16th. I saw nothing remarkable in the Carthusian convent but the sagravio, as they call it, which is well inlaid with different sorts of marble.[85] The view from it is very beautifull. It commands the whole Vega which is full of gardens and plantations. There is a handsome hospital here that is dedicated entirely to the pox. The smell of the rooms they lie in is intolerable.

An Irish officer told me that the pay of a Colonel in the Spanish service was twenty five pistoles a month, but that the Irish colonels had thirty five

---

84 The Alhambra was the palace-fortress of the last Moorish kingdom in Spain. The Court of the Lions was in the heart of the harem. Sixteen princes of the Abencerraje family were murdered when their chief, Hamet, fell in love with Zoraya, the Sultan's favourite.

85 The Carthusian monastery at La Cartuja is one of the most lavish baroque churches in Spain.

pistoles a month more. A captain has a Spanish crown a day. Their Companys are review'd once a month and, if they are complete, they have a certain gratification.[86]

The jurisdiction of the chancelleria of Grenada has a great extent; it takes in all between the Tagus and the Mediterranean. They have one court particularly destin'd for the disputes that happen about their gentility which they call that of the Hijos de Algo.

17th. I observ'd that the lawyers don't stand up when they plead; they sit on a bench rais'd as high as that of the judges. The cathedral is a new building and one of the handsomest in Spain.[87] Joining to it is a chappel where Ferdinand and Isobel, who took this town from the moors, are buried. Near their tomb is that of Philip and Iuana la Loca, their daughter and son-in-law.

Don Gonzalo of Cordova, commonly call'd the Great Captain, is buried near the high altar in the convent of Jeronomites. The church is full of indulgences; one particular to one altar granted, as 'tis said at his request, which (is) that whatever priest says mass there a soul shall immediately be let out of purgatory.

In the evening I went to see some of the Carmines which are little gardens on the side of the Darro.[88] One of them that belongs to a priest is very pretty. It lies just under the Alhambra so he has the advantage of that water with which he has made a very pretty water-works. The source of the Darro is about a league from Grenada. Till it comes into town it runs between two hills that cross near one another that they only give room for the river and little gardens which begin almost at the source of it. These they call Carmines and say that the Moors used to come here from Africa to be cured of calentures[89] for it is always cool there.

18th. I continued in the Vega for two leagues after I left Grenada. After I was out of it I found a sensible change both in the soil and in the cultivation. I din'd at a little place call'd Isnallos five leagues from Grenada. From thence to Guadix, a little city where I lay, is seven leagues thro' mountainous, barren, uninhabited country. We coasted along the range of mountains they call the Sierra Nevada.

19th. I saw but one or two houses between Guadix and Beaca tho' it be seven leagues. I met two travellers, who besides their own guns had three men arm'd with guns to convey them. I lay at Cullar, a little place four leagues further; the country continues mountainous.

---

86 A bonus.

87 The Capilla Real is a flamboyant, gothic cathedral built in the first decades of Christian rule as a mausoleum for the city's liberators.

88 The Carmines were the Sultan's gardens. The Carmino de las Cascadas, possibly that observed by Lord Limerick, is a staircase with water flowing down its stone balustrades.

89 A calenture is a hot, tropical fever.

20th. From Cullar to Velez is eight leagues. The road lies thro' little valleys that are tolerably fruitfull. The moors had a castle upon a rocky hill just by the town.

21st. Lorca, the first town I pass'd thro' of the Kingdom of Murcia, is seven leagues farther.[90] The road to it lies thro' a wild mountainous country. The situation of the town is very romantick. It stands on the side of a hill shap'd almost like a sugar loaf, and on the top there is a large moorish castle. There is a handsome collegiate church. I saw a miraculous picture that the Friar told me work'd miracles every day. The sides of the walls are covered with waxen arms, legs etc. and a great deal of plaited hair. Here the mountainous road ends and there begins a valley that widens all the way to the Huerta of Murcia. I lay at Totana a village four leagues from Lorca.

22nd. Murcia is eight leagues from Totana. The country hereabouts has suffer'd much from want of rain for some years so they get most of their corn from La Mancha. The cathedral of Murcia is handsome.[91] There is a tower joining to it from whence I had the most beautifull prospect that can be imagin'd of the huerta. It looks indeed like one continued garden & the mountains shape it like an amphitheatre. It seems to have one opening which is the road to Valencia. For, as the valley from Lorca does not lie in a direct line, the plain of Murcia seems to be clos'd on that side. This is the place in Spain next to Valencia where there are the most silk worms.

23rd. I travelled about two leagues in the valley of Murcia, and then I struck into the skirts of the mountains leaving Orignela and the opening which leads directly to the sea on the right. I din'd at Albaterra, a village that belongs to the Count de Peraleda. There is a handsome hall in an old house of his where are his family pictures. The first of his ancestors, who is there, was left heir to Mary Queen of Arragon in her will. This gentleman is stiled Viscount of Rocaberti by the Grace of God, and they say that he is the only nobleman in Spain that is stiled so. Elche, three leagues farther, is a pretty, clean town. I struck out of the road to Valencia to see Alicant which is about four leagues from Elche. Alicant is situated at the foot of a high rock on which stands the castle. It is a small town and not better for the war. When the trench blew up part of the rock they destroyed a great deal of the town. There is a little mole and the road is reckon'd safe.

90 Murcia was a semi-autonomous region of Spain. Although largely desert it was much fought over in ancient times and then controlled by the Moors for 500 years. Huerta is a plain.

91 Murcia cathedral is a mixture of styles known as Mediterranean gothic.

TRANSLATIONS OF LORD LIMERICK'S TRAVEL AND OTHER DOCUMENTS

Don Antonio de Pro, Secretary to our Lord the King and Senior Notary of the Council, and Mayor of this most Noble and Royal City of Cadiz: certifies that by Divine Mercy this said City, and its environs, are free from Plague and other Contagions, praying freely, and certifying more places where notices are presented in conformity with the Laws of the Magistrates, and at the behest of the Count of Limerick of the English Nation, with two servants carrying two suitcases of clothes, they may enter the City square.

Given by the Prefect in Cadiz on the twenty ninth day of March seventeen hundred and twenty three.

His Excellency Lord Count of Limerick, referred to overleaf, arrived at this City with his two servants and was admitted to pass, and leaves now for Estrapona and Marbella on the Royal City Boat wearing his dress clothes, and to whom it may concern he is leaving this City and its surroundings which are free of any contagious disease, as also is the City of Marbella and its surroundings.

I give this letter signed by my hand in Gibraltar the fourth day of April, seventeen hundred and twenty three.

DON JOSEPH CARRILLO de ALBORNOZ, Count of Montemar, Knight of the Order of Santiago, Commander of Moratalla of the same Order, Lord of Honour of Salillas, Burxaman and Armalech, Lieutenant General of His Majesty's Army, General Inspector of the Spanish Cavalry and Interim General of the Army and Principality of Cataluna, etc.

We grant a free and safe passport to – The Count of Limerick, Lord of England, to pass with his two servants to the Kingdom of France. Having heard the circumstances Send orders to the Commander of the Barracks of Cavalry to give an escort of four horses for his personal security.

And we order and command all the Ministers of War and Justice under our jurisdiction, and we ask the ones that are not, to create no impediment to this journey and to give as a favour any help that they may need, in the service of his Majesty. Given in Barcelona: 13th May 1723.

By command of S.E.

THE MOST NOBLE MAYOR OF THE CORPORATION, and Aldermen of this City of BARCELONA, on the 15th May 1723 ————————————
On behalf of this City which is free (by God's Grace) of plague and all bad contagions and all those places that fall under the King's rule, for Gerona

The Count of Limerick, Lord of England and with two servants.

Age: 25

Height: Tall

Hair: Wig

Beard: Thick

Distinguishing features: Blue eyes

Estravan Serra y Vitera
By Order of the Noble Corporation of this City.
Francisco Serra, Secretary.

THE MOST NOBLE MAYOR OF THE CORPORATION and the Aldermen of this City of GERONA on the 17th May 1723.

The Count of Limerick, Lord of England with two servants.

On behalf of the City which is free (by God's Grace) of plague and all bad contagions as are those places that fall under the King's Rule, for France.

Age: 25.

Height: Tall

Hair: With a wig

Beard: Thick

Distinguishing features: Grey eyes

By Order of the noble Corporation of this City
Miguel Bila

JUBILEE OF THE FULLEST

Plenary, perpetual and new Indulgencies granted by N.SS. P. Pope Clemente XI on the days of 10th and 12th July 1717 to the reverent supplicants of the confraternity of the blessed souls of purgatory here in the parochial church of Lord Santiago of this city of Alcalá.

All persons that have Confessed and taken Communion will visit the parochial church of Lord Santiago of this City from Sunday 7th of November eve until sunset when the Brothers of the confraternity of the Blessed Souls will celebrate the funeral obsequies for all the deceased and impore God for the exaltation of the Holy Catholic Church for the rooting out of heresies, and the coming together of Princes and faithful Christians and that they may gain the fullest jubilee and remission of all their sins.

On the other hand, all the Brothers of the said confraternity, and also the men and women who have Confessed and taken Communion, will visit the said church and beg God for the exhaltation of the Holy Mother Catholic Church. For all of Monday 8th of this present month we grant plenary Indulgencies and on Sunday 7th and Tuesday 9th, seven years and seven Lents Pardon, and also sixty days of Indulgence for carrying out any pious work, or praying five times the "Our Father" and the "Hail Mary" for all the deceased members of the said confraternity

All the said Indulgencies and the Jubilee can be dedicated by the Brothers of the confraternity, in their private prayers, for the souls in Purgatory for whom their prayers are intended.

To all the priests who would like to go to this church to say Mass for the Blessed Souls on the Sunday, Monday or Tuesday mentioned above will be given three Reales of charity money.

Preacher will be Fr Andreas de la Cruz – shoeless friar and resident preacher of Toledo.

Given by the Seal of the Holy Cross

QUALIS
INCEPTO
AB